DREAMING
& WAKING

DREAMING & WAKING

The Functional Approach to Dreams

Richard Corriere, Ph.D.
Werner Karle, Ph.D.
Lee Woldenberg, M.D.
Joseph Hart, Ph.D.

PEACE PRESS

Copyright © 1980 by Richard Corriere, Werner Karle, Lee
Woldenberg and Joseph Hart

Peace Press, Inc.
3828 Willat Avenue
Culver City, California 90230

9 8 7 6 5 4 3 2 1

Printed in the United States of America by Peace Press.
Typesetting by Freedmen's Organization, Los Angeles.

Library of Congress Cataloging in Publication Data
Main entry under title:

Dreaming & waking.

  Bibliography
  Includes index.
  1. Dreams. 2. Psychotherapy. I. Corriere,
Richard.
BF1091.D73   154.6'3   80-21876
ISBN 0-915238-41-1 (pbk.)

The authors wish to acknowledge the following for permission to reprint from their works:

American Anthropological Association: excerpts from "Dreams and the Wishes of the Soul: A Type of Psychoanalytic Theory among the 17th Century Iroquois" by Anthony Wallace; appearing in *American Anthropologist.* By permission of the American Anthropological Association and the author.

Basic Books, Inc.: excerpts from *The Interpretation of Dreams* by Sigmund Freud (1960 Edition). Reprinted by permission of the publisher.

Mrs. Clara Stewart Flagg: material from the works of Kilton Stewart reprinted by permission of his widow, Mrs. Clara Stewart Flagg. 11645 Chenault Street, Los Angeles, CA 90049. All rights reserved.

Princeton University Press: excerpts from *The Collected Works of C.G. Jung,* edited by Herbert Read, Michael Fordham, Gerhard Adler, William McGuire; translated by R.F.C. Hull. Bollingen Series XX, © by Princton University Press. Reprinted by permission.

Unichappell Music, Inc.: lyrics from *Sh-Boom (Life Could Be a Dream)* by James Keyes, Claude Feaster, Carl Feaster, Floyd F. McRae and James Edward. Copyright © 1954 by Progressive Music Publishing Co., Inc. All rights controlled by Unichappell Music, Inc. (Rightsong Music, Publisher) All rights reserved. Used by permission.

*We dedicate this book to our community of friends,
who make our lives and dreams come true.*

ACKNOWLEDGMENTS

We thank our friends, who lived through the dreams and events that led to this book. We thank our patients, who changed along with us. We thank Sam Mitnick, our former editor at Dell and Harcourt Brace Jovanovich, for his enthusiasm.

We thank our agents, Mr. Michael Gross and Mr. George Kemptner, who helped get this book into print.

We thank Vicki Switzer, who proofread the manuscript. We also thank Nina Solomon, who did a conscientious job of typing the manuscript.

Alan Switzer, Kathy Sullivan, Dr. Michael Hopper and Kathy Hartshorn substantially added to our work with data analyses and research work. We are grateful for their help.

We thank Konni Corriere and Paul Swanson, therapists who supplied us with clinical examples.

We thank Deborah Lott, our editor, and everyone at Peace Press for their efforts.

CONTENTS

1

THE DISCOVERY OF THE TRANSFORMATIVE DREAM

I was parachuting down to a beautiful island in the South Pacific. As I slowly descended I knew that the natives on the island would worship me as a god, that they had a mythology that predicted someone would come from the sky to lead them. Because of this, I knew I could have anything I wanted from them. I also knew that they were an almost perfect culture. They were physically beautiful, loving and free from violence and crime. I knew they needed only one more thing to make their life perfect, and I would bring that to them. Then I was walking up to their village from the beach where I had landed. They were all running toward me and I could see how strong and beautiful they were. I saw them waving to me and I waved back at them. I noticed that I could feel good because they thought I was good and powerful. Then we gathered around a campfire in the village. I suddenly realized what I had that I could give them. It was the final knowledge that they were waiting for and I had it. Just knowing what I was about to say affected me. I could clearly feel inside myself how I was giving up the

false image they had of me. As I gave it up I felt
more and more feeling of power and sadness inside
me. "There are no leaders," I told them. I suddenly
felt much closer to them. I felt a sense of relief go
through my body. I had friends in my life instead of
being separate. I began to cry and told them how
glad I was to be there. As I looked closer, I saw that
they were actually my friends—Steve, Carole, Riggs,
Joe, Dominic, Jerry, Werner—they were all gathered
around me.

This is a transformative dream. It differs from what has
been called "normal" dreaming. Read it slowly; do not, as
yet, attempt to study it or compare it. Do not analyze or explain
it. Read through the dream and notice how it feels. Experience
the shifts in feeling that the dreamer undergoes, from beginning to end. This dream is complete. It needs no interpretation. As it unfolds it tells the dreamer all he needs to know
about himself in terms that are simple and human. It shifts
from symbolism to realism.

This book is about our discovery of this kind of transformative dream and the new functional theory of dreaming that
developed from these dreams. We want to describe our discovery in an intentionally personal and evocative way before
moving to theoretical explanations, and clinical analyses, all
of which follow. Experience should come first and analysis
second.

THE LIMITS OF AN
IMPERSONAL SCIENCE

"I's" and "me's" are avoided in current scientific writing.
Occasionally a scientist might permit himself a quick "I conclude" or "I reasoned" but never "I felt" and never "the solu-

tion came to me." The first person is too subjective and open for the objective scientific style. This was not always true. In the early years of science even chemists and physicists wrote of their work and concepts in a personal way. Their laboratories were their homes. Science was an intrinsic part of the lives of Newton, Curie and Pasteur, as can be seen in the personal way they wrote and the theories they derived.

Theories of dreaming have mainly been formulated by individual therapists who drew upon their own experiences and those of their patients. Each of the major contributors to dream theory, Freud, Jung, Perls, and others, drew a great deal from their own experience in working out their own therapy. It is important for fellow dream researchers to realize that meaningful theories are intimately connected to personal experience. The experience can be applied to other people, but the theory takes on its greatest importance not because of its universality, but because of its initial relevance. Freud's ideas were important to him because they grew out of his own struggle. It is necessary to evaluate the limits of Freudian theory, but it would be folly to overlook in that evaluation the reality of Freud's confrontation with his own dreams.

Because of the personal nature of this process of discovery, any psychological theory is bounded by the personal limitations of its founders and the community from which the theory evolves. For Freud and Jung, the following incident reflects the limitations in the lives of both theorists. As Jung remembered years later:

> . . . I found our relationship exceedingly valuable. I regarded Freud as an older, more mature and experienced personality, and felt like a son in that respect. But then something happened which proved to be a severe blow to the whole relationship.
>
> Freud had a dream—I would not think it right

to air the problem it involved. I interpreted it as best I could, but added that a great deal more could be said about it if he would supply me with some additional details from his private life. Freud's response to these words was a curious look . . . Then he said, "But I cannot risk my authority." At that moment he lost it altogether . . . the end of our relationship was already foreshadowed. Freud was placing personal authority above truth. (Jung, *Memories, Dreams, Reflections,* 1961, p. 158)

There are rigid limits in effect here. Jung unknowingly was as concerned with authority as Freud, for when the authority was gone, so was their association. It was sad that Jung could not have replied: "I am more interested in you than in your maintaining authority. Keep talking about your life." They failed to realize that talking, the process of their communicating, was more important than the content, or the interpretations that they had been sharing until that time. Words, symbols and interpretations composed the whole of their small community, and the limits of their theories as well. Because of these limits, they were never able to make the transition from their intellectual understanding of dreams to transformative dreaming.

OUR LIMITS

Over nine years ago we began to join together as psychologists, counselors and physicians to share ideas, aspirations and science. We had the opportunity to work together and decided while sharing data and ideas, to extend the sharing process into other areas of our lives. We discovered that the way a person dreams is the same as the way he lives. We wanted initially to have special kinds of dreams. We wanted power dreams, lucid dreams, flying dreams. But we were not then prepared to totally change our lives. And because, at first, we could not identify transformation in our lives, we could not identify transformation in our dreams.

For a while, therefore, we put our study of dreams aside and attempted to push our own individual and group psychotherapy beyond the limits we had experienced up to that time. We became more interested in the completeness of our lives and the lives of our patients.

We—the authors—have many roles. We are "therapists," "scientists," "husbands," "friends," "athletes." When we began working together we had a working scientific and professional relationship. But who we thought we were and how we acted did not often match the way we felt inside. In fact, we were sometimes more comfortable when working together, and less comfortable when socializing. As we began to want to know more about ourselves, we found we were tied to certain roles. We could speak of each other as being "moody," "brilliant," or "understanding" but we were talking about our exteriors. We wondered if there was more to us than the way we acted.

We found that to stop living from these roles brought chaos.[1] This personal chaos led to new thinking about therapy, and dreaming, that was striking. Dreams had often seemed chaotic, but now the chaos began to make sense. We came to the hypothesis that *the imaging that we did in waking was the same as we did when we were asleep.* We were willing to suggest this because as we found ourselves imaging less, we made a discovery. After all the patients were seen and the research papers put aside, we would always return home and face another night of sleep and dreams—our own dreams. A surprising thing began to happen. While alone at night, because of the new approach we had taken in our daily lives and personal therapy, a different dream began to make its appearance.

At first we could only remember a fraction of our new nighttime experiences. But the powerful feelings of those dream fragments lingered long after waking. It began to seem as if every dream, every fragment of every dream, every feeling remembered in the morning, could be used by us in waking. The experience of this new dream was powerful enough to begin to break symbolic waking images and leave each of us with a new and deeper understanding of ourselves.

The dream became clearer as we took new parts in our own dreams. We became dreamers who were active instead of passive. We began destroying dream symbols through our own action and expression while we were dreaming. We awoke with a clearer perception and identifiable feeling rather than with a puzzling mystery. We rediscovered our interest in dreams as we rediscovered emotional parts of ourselves.

Our clinical theory evolved out of these experiences. Our dream theory emerged from our dreams and the ways we talked about them and shared them. After casually relating our dreams to each other over morning cups of coffee, we noticed that our dreams had as much feeling in them as our waking experiences. We went beyond simple reporting and began to share our dream feelings as well.

We noticed that the new ways we were dreaming affected our lives. Our work habits changed; the ways we did therapy changed; our relationships with each other deepened. We talked to people at lectures and seminars in a new tone. As the power of this new dream style became more clear, we began to formulate our experience into a theory. We had discovered what we now call the transformative dream, and the functional theory of dreaming.[2]

THE THEORY OF TRANSFORMATION

We called our therapeutic experience Feeling Therapy.[3] We found that *feeling is a transformative process, whether it occurs*

in a therapeutic session, in waking experience, or in dreaming.
The expression of complete feelings inevitably begins to make a person's feeling life work differently, and this is reflected in his dream life. In our personal therapy, we began by realizing that we often had been withholding parts of ourselves, the unsafe thoughts and expressions we were afraid to reveal. We were sharing incomplete feelings by not matching what was happening internally with what we showed on the outside. As we were more and more able to sense the effects this secrecy had on us, we began to match our external expressions to our internal sensations and meanings. We began to realize that sharing complete feelings was both a terrifying change and an exhilarating chance for something more.

We discovered that a dream was not *just a dream,* but a highly recognizable statement of feeling. And just as in a waking experience, this statement was sometimes complete and other times incomplete, sometimes symbolic, and other times clear and direct. In fact, we found that dreams, when considered as pictures of feelings, showed as much variety of experience as waking life did. There was a parallelism between waking and dreaming.

THE TRANSFORMATIVE DREAM

While an incomplete or "normal" dream needs interpretation to give it some meaning, a completely functional or transformative dream carries with it sufficient meaning, sensation, and expression to tell the dreamer all there is to know about him- or herself in that moment. It reflects the movements toward a fully feeling life that the individual is making each day, and it charts the feeling potential that is within.

Within the functional theory of dreaming we repeatedly stress that the content of a dream is not as important as shifts in the process of expression. These shifts—the number of them and their emotional impact—are what leave the dreamer (and the reader) with a special feeling about the transformative dream. In fact, it is the degree to which these shifts take place that helps determine whether or not a particular dream is transformative.

In the transformative dream, the dreamer takes incomplete feelings and their visual symbolism and through active expression changes them into bodily sensations and nonsymbolic images. What this suggests is startling. Dream work, the symbolic coder that Freud believed created the mystery of dreaming, is undone. The dreamer is left with a complete feeling and an internal understanding. This completed feeling at night reflects a parallel process during the day in which the dreamer is able to break from passivity and enter into the process of sharing feeling. This new dream was functionally different. We did not need analyses or interpretations. The dream became the message. This is a fundamental discovery. We did nothing to the dream. The dream itself was working differently.

Freud described dream work in minute detail. We reformulate to say that dream work keeps the dream from working. Dream work or censorship indicates malfunction. Dream work takes simple daily experiences and mixes them up so they no longer fulfill their function, which is to show how the dreamer is feeling and help him to feel better.

When the transformative process prevails over defensive processes then dreams are not bizarre, mixed-up or confusing. Instead, dreams become direct and realistic expressions of what the dreamer is feeling. *The transformative process is primary and the defensive process is secondary—every dream is potentially a transformative dream.*

In the dream we quoted at the beginning of this chapter the dream is at first strange and bizarre, then, at a certain point, when the dreamer takes action and becomes aware of his real feelings, the dream becomes realistic and direct. We label a dream in which the content remains distorted and the dreamer hidden a *symbolic dream*. A dream which moves from distortion to realism, in which the dreamer is active and expressive and clear and feelingful, is a *transformative dream*.

Most dreams do not work this way. Freud boldly figured out a way to make them work in waking. But making them work while asleep is something else. What transformative dreams show us is how dreams can work and why average dreams do not work. After we discovered how special dreams work, we were able to learn how ordinary dreams malfunction and relate them to therapy.

WAKING AND DREAMING TRANSFORMATION

Therapy sessions can be likened to transformative dreams. In transformative psychotherapy sessions there are shifts from symbolic to direct modes of expression, from confused bits of nonsense to clear meanings about a person's life. We have learned from the transformative dream that the emotional coherence of the session or the dream is what is important. Many therapies are intellectually coherent, but they do not produce transformative dreams. Transformation comes about only through emotional coherence in both waking and dreaming.

Transformation is about the human process which works for a direct representation, in percepts, of feelings. Defenses substitute indirect representations for direct representations.

OTHER DREAMER COMMUNITIES

There are societies less technologically advanced than ours that have produced transformative dreams. These societies were not founded by a single individual, or limited by one personality. They were just communities in which dreams were used to understand and nurture the emotional life of each individual. The Iroquois of America and the Senoi of Malaysia understood the significance of the transformative dream. These cultures shared dream feelings and fostered transformative dreaming. They worked in their communities to enable everyone to share in that type of dream. When a member recalled a transformative dream, the rest of the community recognized it. The Senoi and Iroquois will be discussed further later on. At this time just remember the necessity of community participation in the rationale we are developing about using dreams.

It is not necessary to be far advanced in the sophistications of literature and technology in order to begin to experience the transformative dream. It is necessary, however, to be part of a vital community in which the dreamer is willing to expose his or her feelings to fellow community members, to make oneself public by expressing what is private.

MAKE PUBLIC THE PRIVATE

It is a popular misconception that dreams are necessarily and desirably private, and that once revealed, like some mindless storm, will harm everyone in their path. Privacy supported the authority that existed between Freud and Jung, and then later between Jung and his followers. The distance created by authority constantly disappointed Perls and led to the failure of the Gestalt community that was his final goal. Making public what is private eliminates this distance, and is the foundation for any community that aspires toward transformation in waking and dreaming. In this manner the community is both a requisite and a result, a tool and a goal. In an intentional community, the public sharing of feelings allows full contact among community members.

This contact is both reflected and prescribed as the community member begins to work through all the disguised symbols and characters in his or her dreams and to dream transformatively. The member begins to feel the contact that has already been enjoyed, and is shown the deeper feeling contact that is still his or hers to attain.

The choice is not whether to be part of a community. Everyone belongs to a community, not just primitive tribes in past or distant lands. The house you live in, the neighbors, the place you work, all constitute some sort of a community. What happens in such an unrecognized and unchosen community is that the basic prerequisites for transformative dreaming and living are not followed. The private is not made public. In fact, the opposite is often true, the private can not be made public.

In unintentional communities, there are many unspoken thoughts and unexpressed feelings. One consequence of these communities is that to make sense out of what is happening you must interpret. It begins the first time you have to guess what other people are feeling because they are withholding. It begins for a child when he or she must learn to interpret what a parent's silence, or inappropriate responses, really mean. By the time the child has matured into an adult dreamer, his or her ability and need to interpret are fully developed. In effect, overinterpretation develops from making sense instead of having and showing feelings.

DREAM COMMUNITY AND DREAM SCIENCE

Most discoveries are not intentional. What is intentional, however, is the way they are used after they have been made. We discovered the transformative dream during our search for a personal and intensive psychotherapy. Being dream researchers, we wanted to measure it, share it and replicate it. But we found that the uniqueness of the dream made this very difficult. We had more questions than answers. How do you put feeling into words? How can you statistically describe the emotional impact of the transformative dream? What kinds of graphs do you draw to describe the movements from symbolism to complete expression that occur in these dreams? In fact, how do you define and determine symbolism, movement and expression?

Since dream research was already over fifty years old, we hoped we could find what we needed in the existing literature. Unfortunately, that hope was not realized. What we found instead was that dream research has remained tied to Freud. What is said (the content of the dream) has become more important than how a person is saying it (the process of the dream). We changed this emphasis. The basic shift of focus, in the functional approach to dreams, is from the dream symbols or content of the dream to the dreamer. In short, we look at *the way the dreamer is functioning in the dream.* This basic shift frees us from the need to figure out what the symbols mean. Instead, we can clearly evaluate how effective or in-effective the dreamer is in any single dream. We can also look for patterns and consistencies in the way the dreamer functions emotionally across a series of dreams. In the same way we can evaluate the relationships between waking functioning and dream functioning. And we can connect the dreamer's night-time community, and how he or she functions in it, to the way the person functions in his or her daytime community.

We became intrigued with the beauty of the dream itself and how it worked. We defined these interworkings as "process." The dream *as reported* is part of the dreamer's process. We are not so bold as to say the dreamer could or should report it any other way. We accept it as is. We found that as patients became more experienced, they carried more and more of the way their dream affected them into waking. This was reflected in the way the dream was reported. Rather than try to develop a machine that would circumvent the dreamer, we realized that to try and establish such a separation would be bad for dream research. The television of dreams would not lead any-where new unless dreamers began to broadcast new and better programs.

This enabled us to stop looking at what the dream said, what it meant, what it looked like, at how many objects were in it. We de-emphasized content. By developing a few simple methods of personality analysis we were able to see how effective dreamers function, our key research interest. We were able to describe the personality profile of transformative dreams. This profile gives the researcher and the reader a clear picture of the way a dreamer functions emotionally. This book offers to the reader a new way of looking at dreams, to the researcher a new way to do dream research, to the clinician a new insight into what direction dream therapy can take, and finally, most importantly, *Dreaming and Waking* shows how dreams can be culturally developed.

PRACTICAL ADVICE FOR USING DREAMS

This book is not primarily a manual for the personal use of dreams.[4] However, you may find that applying the theory experientially will help you to understand the functional approach to dreams. Here are some suggestions for applying the functional method.

How to Remember Dreams. There are many methods people can use for remembering dreams but there is one special method that is best in keeping with the functional approach because it requires the dreamer to become active immediately. This method is called *Priming*. When you awaken in the morning, even if you cannot remember a dream, ask yourself, *"How do I feel?"* And then, sometime later in the morning, while you are showering or eating breakfast, or preparing for work, actually make up a dream related to the way you felt when you first woke up. The daydream you make up should be complete with pictures and dialogue. If you were feeling sad, make up a sad dream. If you were feeling angry, make up an angry dream. If you were frustrated, make up a frustrating dream, and so on.

The *Priming* method will help you to pay attention to the stuff that dreams are made of, feelings and pictures. Usually within a week, if you follow this method, you will begin to remember your dreams spontaneously.

The Daily Use of Dreams. There are three basic starter questions that can be applied to any dream to alert you to the way you function. Ask yourself:

1. *"How do I feel in this dream?"*
   Be sure you start by asking this question immediately so that you will not be led away from the feelings of the dream into a preoccupation with the symbols.

2. *"Am I the main character in this dream?"*
   This question will orient you to pay attention to how you are and what you do. After all, no one else can influence you or force you to dream a certain way, so if you are dreaming of yourself as a spectator or as a victim, you need to become aware of the role you are creating for yourself.

3. *"How can I change this dream so that I feel better?"*
   This question should be applied when you are not satisfied with how you feel or how you were in the dream. Actually make up some new endings or imagine some new actions that make the dream feel better.

By asking these questions and taking an active attitude toward dreams in the morning, you will prevent "dream hangovers" from dominating the way you feel during the day. You are also preparing for a transformative dream at night. Notice that these methods are applied in the morning. They should *not* be applied at night before going to sleep in an effort to control dreams. The programmatic approach to dreams usually just results in a disruption of sleep; it is not the same as the functional method which works in the morning to change the way you respond to your day.

The Long-term Use of Dreams.

1. When a dream seems particularly powerful or important to you write it down in a dream journal. Don't try to write down every dream or you will make hard work out of something that should be easy and natural.

2. Be sure to talk about your important dreams with friends just as you would talk about anything else of importance that happened to you.

3. Begin to ask the three questions: *"How do I feel?" "Am I the main character?"* and *"How can I change this so that I feel better?"* in regard to experiences in your life as well as about your dreams. You will then begin to connect your nighttime world of feeling with your daytime world. You will see that the way you act in the real world is closely connected to how you are in the dream world.

2

THE FUNCTIONAL
THEORY OF FEELING

The movements of expression give vividness and
energy to our spoken words. They reveal the thoughts
and intentions of others more fully than do words
which may be falsified. The free expression by outward signs of an emotion intensifies it. On the other
hand, the repression, so far as this is possible, of all
outward signs softens our emotions . . . We have
also seen that expression in itself, or the language
of the emotions, as it has sometimes been called, is
certainly of importance for the welfare of mankind.
(Darwin, 1965, *The Expression of Emotions in Man
and Animals,* pp. 364–66)

For the past forty years research has attempted to expand
psychological formulations to include cognition within learning
theory. The Cognitive Drive[1] denotes the drive to collect and
organize sensory information. It is primarily concerned with
what comes into the organism, whether primate or human.
As Harlow's (1950) experiments indicate, monkeys seem to
have a desire to receive sensory stimulation without any further
reward; they could press buttons to get food, sex, or receive
sensory information and chose the latter. He therefore assumed
that the monkey simply enjoyed mental stimulation, and so
he referred to cognition as a basic drive.

THINKING AND FEELING

We distinguish between *thinking* and *knowing*. The Cognitive Drive is often subtly expanded to include one's desire "to know." There is a difference. We are not interested in *what* a person is thinking, just *that one thinks*. We make this distinction because the logic behind "knowing" implies that some higher value, some selective information necessary for the enjoyment or even the survival of life, results from knowing. But every therapist is aware that thinking is not always a good thing. It doesn't always feel good, nor does it always work. We recognize that people do have a drive to think, but often think when they don't need to, about things they don't need to think about, in ways that are self-destructive.

We find it is time to return to something overlooked and even more basic. What does it *feel* like to think? Does cognition always contribute to human welfare?

Expression has been de-emphasized. Over 100 years ago, Charles Darwin emphasized the importance of expression for the welfare of humanity. The author who popularized the concepts of survival of those animals with the greatest adaptive capacity stressed that expression was among man's supreme talents. People have since misconstrued Darwin's ideas to infer that the human advantage is based solely on our cognitive ability. The ability to express feeling has been overlooked both theoretically and personally.

It is ironic that the expression of feeling has become secondary in past and current theories of dreaming and dream functioning, because Freud himself was an avowed evolutionist. But when Freud says, "What is the hidden message in the dream?" he asks for an answer that can be supplied by our cognitive powers, and our ability to interpret. The questions "How does this dream feel?" and "How is the dreamer expressing feelings in the dream?" relate to our ability and drive to express, and have been overlooked.

THE AFFECTIVE DRIVE

We believe the expression of feeling to be a drive and we term it the Affective Drive. The effect of this drive on dreaming will be shown to be both powerful and valuable in terms of human survival. It is time to stress the expression of feeling, to study, theorize, and test those theories concerning feeling and its expression regardless of the fact that it is subjective and thus difficult to measure. We want to establish a balance in dream research and dream theory that has been lacking from the beginning. In doing this we are only adding to what has already gone before. If we find Freud biased toward knowing your dreams we present a balancing bias toward feeling your dreams.

When we talk about feelings, we are not referring to private thoughts, emotional outbursts, physical sensations, or danger-ous impulses. These are common conceptions and miscon-ceptions of what feelings are (See Hart, Corriere and Binder, 1976, *Going Sane: An Introduction to Feeling Therapy*). By feeling we mean *integral* feelings: a sensation and its meaning completely expressed so that what a person experiences inter-nally is matched in intensity to what he or she reveals.

Other definitions of feeling consider them as pure sensory input (Titchener as discussed in Schultz, 1960) or include cog-nitive organization (Miller et al., 1960; Gendlin, 1962). All these definitions are similar in that the experiencing of what they call a feeling or perception and the expression of that feel-ing are considered two different things. In other words, a person can be accurately and fully feeling whether or not he or she chooses to express. We disagree.[2]

Our definition reflects the *public experience* of a person who is feeling. Expression is not distinct from feeling, but is part of the experience. Darwin is stating an important general-ization when he says, "The free expression by outward signs of an emotion intensifies it. On the other hand, the repression, so far as this is possible, of all outward signs softens our emotions" (Darwin, 1965, pp. 364-66). Part of the feeling is the further self-awareness of your own body movements as you express. Without this awareness, the experience dissipates.

When expression is less, then the sensation is less, because without movement there is no physical stimulation. Without expression there can be no confirming response from the immediate environment. The loss of all this sensation results in an imbalance of meaning. The cognitive function assumes too great a proportion.

COGNITIVE BALANCE

When we describe integral feelings, we are describing an ideal state in which all sensation and meaning is expressed. People do not live their lives expressing everything. There is a *threshold of privacy* which determines the level of expression. When this threshold is set too high, the cognitive imbalance is too great for satisfactory communication. The threshold must be low enough so that most sensations and meanings of sufficient energy are shared and not privately held.

Here is an example of cognitive imbalance. It presents a process of repression, and although a special case, the process itself is a general one.

> *I awoke feeling a little frightened. My stomach was tight. Jean went to work and I was alone in the house. We had had a fight the night before, and she had not said good-bye that morning like she usually does. As the morning progressed I got more and more depressed. I started thinking about my job, how boring it was. I was worried about our marriage. I drove to the store and even the car seemed too old. It wasn't exciting to drive though it was new.*

In this case the unshared sensation became generalized into depression. Soon everything experienced was at such a low level of feeling that all that remained were cognitive associations. These associations were not based on an expressive person dealing with the present environment. The associations, depressing in their own right, made him feel even worse. He is suffering from a cognitive imbalance and his feeling life is incomplete.

A complete or integral feeling exists when two conditions are met. First, the expression must be carried through until the sensation is above the threshold of privacy. Second, the feeling must be ordered, or free of the past associations that are not presently useful. In the previous example the first requirement, complete expression, was not met. As a result the second requirement, ordering, became even more difficult to achieve. As the morning progressed, more and more associations, unconsciously derived from past experience, intruded on his present life until a boring, worried and depressed condition was prominent.

Our definition of a complete feeling represents a balance between expression and cognition. Incomplete feelings represent an overworking of cognition so that the feeling is distorted, or disordered. But what form do incomplete feelings take? As we shall see, the imbalance of feeling and thinking results in the formation of images.

An image is a representation of a feeling to which thought has been added. We could call it a *feeling thought*. For instance, if you look at a book, it is a combination of sensations (size, shape, color) plus meanings. The meanings are made up of past associations that suggest it is a book. If you close your eyes you can imagine the book. You have added another thought process (picturing the book) to your original partial sensation. By definition, when there is thinking substituting for expression, we have imaging. Images can substitute for feelings when expression is either absent or inadequate.

The cognitive functioning represented by imaging has a

definite value for survival, both historically for man through the centuries, and personally for each individual as he or she matures from infancy. It is a natural function of our central nervous system, and can be used, or in many cases, misused. The following is an account of Hunter's classical experiments on delayed responding conducted over forty-five years ago. It helps us to see how images can work for our welfare as well as against it.

In his experiment, Hunter compared the cognitive functioning of a chicken and a dog. A female chicken, twenty-six weeks old, could see a dish of corn placed six feet in front of her. She was separated from the dish by a clear pane of glass five feet wide. The chicken was hungry, and she repeatedly rushed at the food, striking the glass with such ferocity that she soon lost consciousness. The chicken is unable to form an image. She lacks the level of cognitive functioning necessary to change the visual sensation or picture of the corn to image form. She can not make an internal or mental representation. Acting just on what she sees, she repeatedly propels herself into the glass. She is mentally unable to walk around the barrier.

An animal with greater cognitive functioning is able to go further distances, and do intermediate tasks in order to reach the food. A female dog, twenty-six weeks old, could see a dish of meat six feet in front of her. She was separated from the dish by a clear pane of glass five feet wide. The dog was hungry and she walked around the pane of glass and ate the meat. Substituting images for feelings confers an advantage to the dog. But the human is able to image more effectively than any other animal. We can delay responses through intermediate tasks and images to plant corn in the spring for a fall harvest and a future winter's dinner. Obviously, imaging can work for our own welfare. In the following section we will see how it can work against it.

DISORDERING

A child maturing in his home quickly learns to substitute images for feelings. Surrounded by adults with fully developed cognitive functioning, a child's affective drive is easily overcome. It is as though the immature human and the mature human were two different animals. Of the two, the child is more in balance, with few impeding memories and past associations to infringe on present feelings. We call the process by which the child learns to substitute imaging for his own exploration and sensation, *disordering*.

The following example demonstrates how everyday disordering occurs.

A little girl and her father were in a restaurant standing near the cash register. She saw some peppermint candy sticks in a glass jar and this conversation took place:

Girl: I want some candy.

Father: [*No response*]

The daughter expresses herself, and there is a lack of confirming response by the father—either a "yes" or a "no" would have at least related to her expression.

Girl: What is it? [*Points at candy*]

Father: [*No response*]

Again there is a lack of confirming response, and in this case it leads to an unnecessary cognitive function. The daughter is asking a question in lieu of expressing.

Girl: Daddy, what is that? What is that? [*Pulling his sleeve*]

Father: You have had enough sweets today. [*He pulls away*]

The father makes an inappropriate response. He feels uncomfortable with the physical contact initiated by his daughter, and pulls away, without expressing himself.

Girl: But what is it? [*Pointing to the red and white striped candy*]

Father: Oh, it's licorice.

Girl: What is licorice?

Father: Where is your mother?

Girl: I want one.

Father: Oh, all right, but it is bad for your teeth.

This brief exchange, repeated in different ways at different times throughout a childhood, shows how little reality the child receives. Her natural responding process is being disordered, in this case by an adult who quite obviously has unexpressed feelings of his own preoccupying his mind. But by not responding, inappropriately responding, by forcing the child to resort to more and more cognitive functioning, he is laying the foundation for adult disordering patterns and image formation. The girl gets attention, but not a response. The father gives in, but he does not give. When the child matures, she may substitute food or candy for contact, and questions for expressions, as her imaging reflects the cognitive substitutions.

The father is passing on his own inability to respond, make contact, and express. There is no trauma in this scene, only an unremitting and everyday reasonable insanity. In this way the disordering patterns are passed on from generation to generation. The relation between trauma and disorder is acknowledged, but trauma is not the staple diet of childhood; it is extraordinary. But it is the ordinary which drives the hardiest child into emotional disorder, a life with less expression, incomplete feelings, and the symbolism of imaging.

Through reward, punishment, imitation and verbal communication, the child builds a legacy of associations inherited from her adult environment that she will carry into adulthood. And she will carry them into an adulthood that in many cases no longer requires them. The associations and images will not be practical. Whenever thinking substitutes for expressing, past associations begin to disorder her present feeling. Upon final maturity, she will form a family and pass on these disordering patterns to her own offspring.

Every image, no matter how complicated, contains within it some unexpressed feeling. We can see how this feeling gets distorted. Each level of cognitive functioning adds to the symbolism for each represents a past association that may not be useful in the present situation. In the case of the father and his child, the child adapted to her environment and survived by substituting questions for expressed wants. This was useful in childhood, and ineffective in adulthood. Behavior that was adequate for her early life environment became largely symbolic for her as an adult.

When cognitive functions are added unnecessarily to an adult's images, the past associations overwhelm the present partial feeling, just as in childhood. The daytime behavior becomes largely symbolic as the expression becomes more and more indirect. Life becomes a series of daytime images. This image expansion is concurrent with feeling contraction.

We say living is feeling based on the experience of our own lives. We can feel what it is like to think, when it is pleasurable and when it is painful. We remain in the present. We experience it. But we cannot think what it is like to feel. Because, when we do, we are relying solely on past experience and past feeling. We leave the present, and all experiencing stops. We re-experience.

The problem becomes regaining an ordered feeling life once disordering has taken place. Incomplete feelings were originally created by substituting cognition for expression. They are undone in the opposite manner, by expressing. Repression is undone by expression. By moving toward expression, we slowly move from symbolic feelings to primary ones. And as we express, we increase our sensation—much as Darwin stated long ago. Feeling itself is transformational.

We apply the word transformation only when a person shifts from a mixed-up way of living in the world, to another based on the way he or she feels inside. When people begin to completely express integral feelings to other people, they transform their lives. Transformation is not synonymous with change. People can change by imitation, by acceding to outside pressure, by pretending, and by accident. We make no naive claim about the ease of achieving transformation. But we have discovered a process already at work that makes the journey of transformation both possible and natural. We rediscovered dreaming.

After re-establishing the dominance of expression in our waking lives we were free to experience the power and clarity of this expression in our dream lives as well. We returned to our interest in dreams only after experiencing a new kind of dream, and a way of dreaming that we had tried for and failed to accomplish years before. We discovered that dreaming is transformational. And it was the transformational dream that told us.

3

THE FUNCTIONAL THEORY OF DREAMING

Life could be a dream — sh-boom,
If I could take you up in paradise up above —
 sh-boom,
If you would tell me I'm the only one that you love,
Life would be a dream, sweetheart.

(James Keyes et al, *Sh-Boom*, 1954)

Almost everyone seems to agree at least on one thing—a dream is a wish. The definition, while correct in special cases, is too narrow. A dream is usually more than a wish. *A dream is both a feeling and a picture of a feeling*—not merely a wish or a want, but any feeling. A dream is composed of a series of images and feelings, or as we defined previously, feeling-thoughts and feelings. The range of feeling represented visually in dreams is as great as our range of feeling during the day. Every movement toward or away from feeling expression may be found in some form at night.

Dreams are not necessarily mysterious, coded messages from the unconscious. They do not need to be controlled, interpreted, and most of all, they should not be dismissed as unimportant. They are like photographs of feelings and feeling processes. Some of these photographs are more blurred than others, but if you look at them closely you will find the feelings within. Dreams are representative of the unconscious only to the degree we are unconscious of the way we disorder our expressions.

THE PARALLELISM OF DREAMING AND WAKING

Dreaming and waking are not separate states of consciousness. The ways in which we are aware of our feelings, the meanings we attach to them, and the ways we express or repress feelings, are the same at night as they are during the day. In short, while we are sleeping, we have the same affective and cognitive drives and abilities we have during the day. The dreamer and the waking person are the same. The expression of affect in dreams parallels the expression of affect in waking.

Dreams are often studied or explained from the point of view that the processes at night are somehow different and more symbolic than during the day. Dream pictures are supposed to represent secondary information that has been changed or censored from socially unacceptable wishes (usually sexual) into disguised symbolic pictures. We disagree. While sleeping, the dreamer watches the way he or she disguised feeling and lived through images during the day.

A dream of a thirty-five-year-old electrical engineer exemplifies this parallelism. He entered therapy in the midst of a divorce proceeding that was breaking up his family. The feeling he was having was interfering with his work, and his usual stolid and unemotional exterior was under attack. Throughout the early part of his therapy he resisted expressing his feelings for many reasons—feelings were either embarrassing or insignificant, expressing would not change anything, and he had a fear of being reprimanded or ridiculed. Full of held-in anger and sadness, he tried repeatedly to convince his therapist that he had nothing to express. Though the content of these reasons varied, the process remained the same: *I can't show you how I feel.* Two weeks after the beginning of therapy he had the following dream fragment.

I am walking down a large street with an old trench coat on. I have lots of fruit and vegetables in special pockets concealed inside the coat. A friend asks me for something to eat. I reach in my pocket and hold out an old apple core.

He had not begun to change in any dramatic way, but he was becoming aware of how he disguised his feelings during the day. The process of concealment was appearing in his dreams. He was being helped to notice how he lived through images instead of giving his concealed feelings to his friend. His dream was not more symbolic than his waking behavior. Why dreams are symbolic should now be evident. Dreams are symbolic because waking is symbolic. Just as one can have a balance or imbalance between cognitive and affective states while awake, so can one when dreaming. Symbolic dreams represent the cognitive overload at night.

The cognitive associations that seem so reasonable during the day ("I cannot show how I feel because . . .") seem bizarre when seen visually at night. During the day, the cognitive drive overwhelms the affective drive. The way we disorder our feelings, therefore, often seems to make sense. We make sense by having thoughts instead of "having sensations." At night this changes—the cognitive drive weakens while the affective drive begins to ascend, making our ways of being symbolic seem bizarre.

While dreaming, the balance is not so much in favor of the cognitive drive. Isolated while sleeping, the dreamer cannot mobilize his environment to help him withhold feeling. He cannot work too hard, keep busy, forget what he is doing, or involve other people in the many different types of struggles and problems that substitute for feeling. All the dreamer can do is remain sleeping, or awaken. If he remains in the dream, the affective drive will begin to work.

THE PRINCIPLE OF COMPLETION

The process of a dreamer's life is continuous. Feelings that have been incompletely expressed during the day are presented at night. Because of the increased affective drive these incomplete feelings try to come to completion during dreaming.

Our completion principle is in line with current research that suggests there is a need to dream (Foulkes, 1966, p. 206). We differ by saying that the need is not based on the "safety valve theory" as postulated by Freud, but on a drive toward expression. This drive to express is distorted during dreaming by the defensive modes (present in waking and dreaming) that override expression. The distortion of this drive decreases as these defensive modes decrease.

There is an impulse to express feelings completely and openly. In short, there is a drive in waking and dreaming that moves toward full consciousness. This basic dream process drives feelings to completion. During the day we call it the affective drive. As we will shortly describe, we call it by another name at night.

Feelings are left incomplete when cognitive functioning *substitutes* for matched expression. During dreaming the opposite process slowly begins to occur. Expression tries to substitute for cognition. It is the body's natural healing system against an unbalanced state. We acknowledge that the body has an immune system to fight infectious disease, and an ability to heal from physical trauma. Dreaming represents this function within the central nervous system. It functions to return the system to wholeness.

Dreaming is feeling, but that feeling can be balanced or unbalanced. Symbolic, unbalanced feeling can work against the disordered person during the day and at night as well. Feelings become so lost in dream symbolism that they no longer work. Far from being a natural function of dreaming, Freud's dream work mechanism or censor, is a representation of the disordering process. It is a secondary process, the acquired cognitive overload working at night. *Dream work keeps the dream from working.*

By labeling the dream work mechanism an acquired function of dreaming, we were free to discover a primary process of dreaming hitherto overlooked. And by redefining "normal" dreaming to be disordered or pathological, we were free to look for higher forms of dream activity that reflected the primary process. The process we discovered was transformation, and the highest form of dream that reflected this process was the transformative dream.

THE PROCESS OF TRANSFORMATION

Transformation is the process of moving from a symbolic mode of dreaming, based on substitute images, to an expressive non-symbolic mode, based on the expression of feelings. It is a primary or innate process which moves the dreamer toward the full active expression and completion of his or her feelings. It is the same process which operates in the waking state as the *affective drive.*

The key to understanding transformation is realizing that it is a process of movement. Dream experience moves from being totally symbolic, passive, confused, without feeling, and lacking human contact, to being nonsymbolic, active, fully clear, full of feeling, and containing human contact. We are concerned here more with dream processes than dream contents—the dreamer's role (sometimes referred to as activity), clarity, expression, feeling, and contact, rather than the number of horses, trees, strangers, environments, and other categories of images. Transformation is concerned with *how* we dream, as well as *what.*

The following are examples of normal dreams. Hall defines the normal dream exerience as one in which the setting is outdoors, the dreamer is passive, hostile, apprehensive, and the dream is unpleasant overall. These dreams are consistent with Hall's prototype except for their indoor settings.

I am in a cleaners. I am waiting in a long line a very long time. My mother, grandmother and friend are in line with me. My friend is very angry. A woman in front of us wants to leave all of my clothes on the counter with a name but I do not want to. I am afraid it will be lost.

C. arrives in Los Angeles from Atlanta for a visit with me. She is very attractive and strange men are often starting conversations with her. I am in a hotel room waiting for her to come back from the bar. I am angry because I have been waiting for her. I see her at the bar talking to strange men. I want to go but she wants to stay. One of the men tries to talk to me. I want C. and I to leave. I leave her and walk alone back to the room very angry. C. follows me and knows I am angry but I don't say anything. I am angry at waiting, and jealous of the attention she gets.

The following is an example of a transformative dream. It illustrates the principle of transformation—that it is possible to shift from a symbolic mode of dreaming into a directly expressive one within the dream and without outside interference or interpretation. The patient who had this dream was formerly a timid and withdrawn woman who rarely talked. She recently began a plant-care business and one of her customers was R., an associate of ours.

I am over at R.'s house watering his plants. He's getting ready to go on a trip and he is busily packing and talking with others. I try to say good-bye but he ignores me and I leave feeling drawn back. Then I am in a car driving to the building where R. works.

*He is doing therapy in a group. I barge right in and
interrupt him. I tell him I am here to say good-bye
to him. I grab him by the arms and we talk. We keep
talking. Then R. says to me, "You are not trying to
say good-bye, you're trying to say hello."*

She liked this dream, and reported that she awoke shaken
from it, seeing the possibility of having more in her life by
saying hello. She found that interesting because she would
always hug her friends when she left their houses. She had
been putting more feeling into saying good-bye and ending
contact than in initiating it. This dream represented a turning
point for her. She was beginning to use her energy to begin
contact, instead of to end contact as she had in the past.
Within the dream she stopped feeling withdrawn and passive,
and became the active force. The dream pictures began to
work for her instead of against her deeper feelings and needs.

We distinguish between transformative dreams and the
functional approach to dreams. The functional approach is a
mode of relating to dreams on the basis of feelings. Our emphasis shifts from the traditional concern about "What does
it mean?" to a concern with the questions: "How do I feel in
this dream?" and "How do I function emotionally in this dream?"

When we give courses about dreams we often use movies,
beginning with symbolic ones in which there is very little or no
direct expression of feeling, and progressing toward movies
in which feelings are more fully expressed. We ask the audience
to notice how one film makes them feel better than another.
We turn then from a discussion of "What does it mean?" to
"How does it affect me?" and "Do I like being affected?" We
want them to realize that they can enhance their experience
of films and dreams by paying attention to the feelings they
experience as well as remembering what happened; long before
they are able to dream transformative dreams, they can apply
this approach to films, dreams, and events in their daily lives.

Transformative dreams emerge from a feeling and functional approach to life. We say that dreaming is transformational. Long before dreamers have a fully transformative dream, they have dreams that represent the changes that will occur. These dreams represent one small part of a larger hologram. As each dreamer uses the movement that comes from the functional approach, the fuller picture of transformation may occur.

The principle of transformation is revolutionary. It states that the dreamer can change his or her own defensive processes while dreaming. Whereas Freud states that the censor is always at work, the transformation principle states that the censor can be overcome. This occurs not through interpretation but through the dynamics of the dreamer's expression, within the dream, and in the morning, in response to the dream.

The highly symbolic dream requires interpretation in order for the dreamer to understand what the dream means. The transformative dream needs no outside interpretation. The dreamer awakes with a feeling and an insight; his dreams are working. We have now come full circle. We began our exploration by stating that we thought change was possible, and that human beings could help each other. We stated our own need for sustaining contact. We turned to the processes of our daily lives and began asking functional rather than content questions. We began a journey, and our greatest discovery was a way of travel. Without knowing it, we were preparing ourselves and our patients for a new way of dreaming as well as a new way of living.

By stressing affective processes during the day, we were bringing our consciousness back into balance. By asking certain functional questions during the day, we were preparing ourselves to ask them about our dreams. We were designing a functional psychotherapy, a therapy and community environment that would sustain the transformative process that occurs at night.

In our therapy we began to emphasize expression at the expense of understanding. The result of this daytime experience was realized in our dreams. When we subsequently looked at the new type of dream that was emerging, we began to see all dreams from a new point of view. We could appreciate the feeling expansion that occurred as the imaging broke down and feeling emerged.

Functional Therapy led us back to the use of dreams. It is a transformative psychotherapy—a therapy that balances the functions of the affective and cognitive drives. We do not claim that it is the only transformative psychotherapy, nor that it is the best. We do claim that it led us to transformative dreaming. We feel that any therapy which claims to be transformative must allow the night to extend into the day. This allows the processes of natural dreaming to infringe upon the secondary processes that disrupt daytime consciousness.

Not every dream we dreamed was completely or even partially transformational, but in most dreams the transformational process was apparent. We learned to live from what this process told us, from the feeling those dreams gave us. We tried to live in ways that would sustain the new intensity of feeling. We believe that for any psychotherapy to claim to be transformative, it must support living from the affect drive found in dreaming. Psychotherapy has to be responsible for the affective education of its patients.

AFFECTIVE EDUCATION

After many years of research and practice, we discovered five basic dream processes: *role, feeling, expression, clarity,* and *contact.* Affective education works first to make the dreamer aware of these five functional processes that support transformation. Second, each of these processes is utilized in a manner allowing the patient-dreamer to begin to feel the affects of disordering in the dream and in the waking life. The individual begins to feel how he or she operates from secondary feelings and pictures of feelings. Third, the patient-dreamer is helped to feel the genesis of the disordering. He or she begins to feel the origin of the past associations that comprise cognitive overload.

Finally, the dreamer is helped to use the processes in a new way, based on that person's own natural or innate expressive and cognitive powers. This new or transformative way of being is not based on some external stimulus (the therapist), but on elements emerging from the patient's dreams, which remain the sole reference for transformation.[1]

DYNAMICS IN DREAMS

Each dream dynamic must be considered by itself. The dreamer's role can vary from a passive one in which the person is an impartial observer of his or her own dream, to the fully active where the dreamer initiates the action and has an affect on the results of the dream. The first question we might ask is simply: How active are you in this dream?

The following is an example of a dream in which the dreamer does not play much of a role.

> *My mother takes H. (my friend) to buy a dog. I am watching them. They pick an older dog with long lashes. I want a young dog.*

This dream is not unusual. It is the kind of dream reported as normal by Hall (1951, p. 62). The next dream shows a dreamer taking more direct action and affecting the dream's outcome.

> *I was walking along the beach and I came upon C. (wife) and D. (friend) kissing and hugging. They were pretending that nothing irregular was going on when I approached them. I walked up to them and beat them both up.*

The dreamer reported awaking feeling "good and strong." For many years he had a recurrent dream in which he viewed a scene similar to the one described above, and would begin to feel horribly weak and helpless. "I would feel totally sunk and would have no voice to say anything in my dream, and would awake feeling the same way—weak and helpless." In this dream the dreamer is acting in a new way. He is very active and uses the action to change the dream instead of allowing the symbolism to expand. We would describe his role as active. It fails to be fully active, because at this point the dreamer's action does not include the expression necessary to make the dream greater. But the transformative elements are obvious.

THE POWER DREAM

The following dream represents one where the dreamer is fully active. Because he was more active than he allowed himself to be when awake, he could exceed the limits of so-called reasonable behavior in his dream as well. This is a hallmark of what are commonly referred to as *power dreams*. They are transformatively reasonable in their ability to free the dreamer from incomplete feelings.

> *I was skiing with my friends. It was a clear sunny day and we were all dressed really well and having a good time. J., L., and I had given some instructions to the others who were all learning different things. We were going down this big, wide main run on the way to the main lodge. Suddenly I went ahead and began to do tricks on my skis that I had never done before. I took a jump and when I got in the air, I decided to fly down the rest of the way. I was gliding through the air very slowly like a big bird. I was screaming and yelling, full of excitement. I flew around the chair lift when I saw some people I knew there. I flew by them slowly and said hello. As I got to the lodge I*

descended slowly to where my friends had gathered
to wait for me. I felt very excited.

The most frequently encountered characteristic of the power
dream is the dreamer taking actions that would normally be
impossible, such as flying, breathing under water, walking
through fires, and moving heavy objects. Many people experience such dreams. They may follow some fully active day or
days. What is desirable is that the dreamer begin to enjoy
using the dream's feeling of power while awake.

Again it is important to stress the process of the dream,
and the power of the feeling in the dreamer's body. The actual
content is merely a representation of the sensation. *What* the
dreamer is doing is clearly secondary to the way he or she is
doing it. With more expression, the content of the dream can
shift, as we will show when we present the transformational
dream. In the following example we can see a continuous shift
taking place in the dreamer as he begins his dream isolated
and afraid, and ends the dream with a solid sense of himself.

I was on a cliff and my friends were down below me.
I couldn't get down. It was very steep and slippery.
I was afraid to move or I would fall. I asked C. (my
therapist) what to do. She only said "Do what you
want!" I knew I couldn't go down, so I decided I had
to go up. I started to climb up, and began to fly. I
was very afraid, unsure of myself flying, that I would
fall and die, so I flew upward out of my fear. I kept
looking for a place to rest and stop. I got higher and
higher. There was only one mountain peak left, and
I stopped and rested with one leg on each side of the
mountain top. I couldn't go any higher without dis-
appearing forever. I was still afraid, but I had to go
down. I felt that if I was able to fly up, perhaps I
could fly down. I was feeling more powerful for hav-
ing flown that high, even though I was afraid of

heights. I began to fly down, and as I did I had tremendous confidence and power. The closer I came to the ground, the more powerful and wise I felt. I flew into a city and landed very solidly. It was a city of the future, like in a science fiction movie. I was so wise I would rule them. I grabbed a man and a woman, and told them that they would rule the city, and that I would help them. That way everyone would be represented. I felt powerful that I could finally move myself, and that no one could move me.

In this case the dream contains both elements of power and transformation. It is often difficult to separate types of dreams into distinct categories. In the dream above, the dreamer experiences an awareness of the power he can obtain when he moves toward people instead of away from them. His therapist, C., had recently been working with him to "do what he wanted, to express what he wants to express," as she put it. By holding himself in check because he pictured disapproval from his friends, he was constantly moving away from them and feeling afraid. This feeling process was pictured perfectly with him isolated on a mountain top unable to go any further. The dream is about his past, and the future the dream holds out to him is dramatic. His final words, "I felt powerful, that I could move myself, and that no one could move me," were an important *internal feeling and cognitive experience* for him. He needs to live from this power to allow the transformative process to change him.

Students of dreaming are often amazed at the power of dreams. Dreams have been used by ancient shamans and modern shamans as well to get us to "dream for power."[2] In actual fact, however, this is a narrow and limited use and appreciation of the power in dreams. The pictures presented to the dreamer in most power dreams allow the dreamer to feel the difference between the way he normally lives his life

and the way he could. They can take him from past disordering
to a future full of power and feeling. We must appreciate the
dream in its context of the dreamer's past and present. Otherwise it becomes an entertainment, much like a magician's
trick. You can wonder how such a trick was done, and have
him demonstrate the trick over and over, but all that will
happen is the excitement and vivid amazement will melt away.
So, too, if the nature of the power dream is abused.

THE "NORMAL" (UNCLEAR) DREAM

Dreams can be completely confusing. The distortion so dominates the dream that the dreamer has little or no awareness
of self. The images seem so unrelated that the dreamer has
difficulty telling the dream as a coherent story. We would term
this type of dream a dream without clarity, and many so-called
"normal" dreams, reported in the literature, are of this nature.

> *I was walking or moving somehow through a woods.*
> *The trees were really made of steel poles but some-*
> *how they were growing. I wasn't sure what, but an*
> *old man told me "business as usual." Everything*
> *melted and I was a dog and was being chased by*
> *something. I didn't really care. I was looking down at*
> *everything. It was very dark.*

THE LUCID DREAM

Dreams are often a mixture of clarity and confusion. There is
some idea of what is happening, but feelings and events seem
disconnected. Occasionally, however, the dreamer has a dream
in which the feelings are clear and direct, the picture makes
sense and there is no distortion. (We call this type of dream
the *lucid dream*.)

> *I was running down a street after some stranger. He*
> *had lost his wallet and I wanted to return it to him.*
> *As I got closer to him, I could feel my whole body*

moving in slow motion. I knew I was dreaming and
I enjoyed the physical sensation. I lost him in a crowd
of people, but it didn't matter since it was a dream.
My sensation seemed more important to me.

The dreamer's statement, "it was a dream," is very important. It allows for change. He is not restricting himself to the content of the dream. He sees that he is dreaming, and that he is free to be the way he wants to be without having to worry about the "meaning" in the dream. This awareness is a signal that the dreamer is allowing for more internal awareness during the day. The dream is lucid.

The lucid dream has been widely discussed in the dream literature. It is normally defined as a dream "in which the dreamer knows he is dreaming and feeling fully conscious in the dream itself" (Tart, 1969, p. 1). Our own definition of this dream is the same as the standard one but we add the phrase "fully aware." The awareness has to allow for a course of action that is beneficial to the dreamer *within the dream*. To be aware that one is dreaming, and not make a choice that allows one to feel more is an example of a clarity that has no value.

The following example shows a dreamer who suffers from a false clarity in waking and dreaming. During waking, he thinks he sees and knows what is happening around him, but his expressive level is so low that he never tests his awareness. During his dream life, his false clarity is visually apparent.

I was in my back yard at home. I had a bicycle but
the handlebars fell off and I couldn't ride it. Some
man handed me a nut to fix it, but it was way too
big. He put it on and it fit, so I got on and started
riding down the highway. I was going very fast, just
by leaning back and holding on to the handlebars.
I wasn't pedaling, and I was passing cars and trucks.
I thought that wasn't possible, that I better pedal
fast, but I could not do it, and each time I tried to

*pedal I slowed down. I gave up trying and just sat
back and enjoyed it.*

What he "knew" and what he was experiencing were different. The dream was about giving up a false clarity and
achieving a clarity based on an active experience. Lucid
dreams are sometimes called "altered states of consciousness."
We contend that the lucid dream is quite natural. We have
found in our clinical work that the more aware a person becomes of his own feelings, the more lucid his or her dreams
become. The following is an example where the awareness of
the dreamer helps him experience the dream.

*R. was acting very crazy and loud. I started moving
toward him very slowly but methodically. As I approached he became louder and I began to feel
scared. Then something happened and I realized
that I was totally separated from R. I was scared,
but the fear was inside me alone, it was my fear and
it was okay. I walked right up to him and held him
while he was yelling. I finally subdued him into being
quiet and soft without me having to say a word.*

This is an example of a dream that is working. The
dreamer is aware of what he feels and then acts on the awareness. He reported feeling strong and wise on awaking. He was
acting instead of reacting to his friend. Those who argue for
the problem-solving function of dreams would relish the
explicit solutions taken in dreams such as this.

In the above dream, incomplete feelings allowed for a
distortion but the dream work wasn't continued. The distortion
mechanism was disengaged because the dreamer's recognition
of his real feeling allowed for action which short-circuited the
dream work. Freud would be hard-pressed to explain these
dreams as wish fulfillments. Wish fulfillment is possible in
symbolic dreams because the dreamer is usually no more active

than he or she was when awake. The dreamer may *get* more, but does not *do* more. One gets passively. But in a transformative dream one experiences a completion of feeling (nonsymbolic in nature) that makes wishing irrelevant.

THE LUMINOUS DREAM

Some dreams have such a low feeling level that they have no effect on the dreamer. In other dreams, feeling is dominant. These we call *luminous dreams.* The dreamer allows him- or herself to be aware of the feeling and permits it to occur to the fullest extent. The pictures the dreamer sees involve expanded images because they contain more feeling than he or she can express. An expanded imagery helps contain the feeling. In the power dream the added feeling is expressed in an expanded physical action.

The luminous dream reveals an increase in the dreamer's feeling level. Such a dream indicates either that the dreamer is ready for and needs an increase of feeling in his or her life, or that such an increase has just occurred. In many cases it embodies both situations. The following two dreams by the same dreamer show how a development of feeling takes place. The dreams occurred in a two month period during which the dreamer underwent significant changes in his life. He was learning how much his thoughts weakened him, and becoming aware of new feeling and the power which resulted. Just at the beginning of this period he had the following dream:

> *I was driving along the ocean. I saw a beautiful bay.*
> *I saw the water was a color blue I had never seen*
> *before. I loved the color, it was magnificent. I saw*
> *palaces and white marble estates built over the water.*
> *I couldn't believe how beautiful it was, or that there*
> *was a blue that color. I awoke from the dream doubt-*
> *ing that such a color could really exist, it was so*
> *fantastic.*

He was so unused to the new feeling (in this case represented by a new color) that his thoughts ended the dream.
His awareness of feeling was not complete, and the self-doubts
and rational thoughts of the past were enough to destroy the
image. He reported intense pleasure looking at the scene. The
only reason to end the dream was the unreasonableness of the
disordering process. Two months later, having continued to
experience how much his thought processes weakened him and
how living with feeling gave him strength, he had the following
dream:

> I was out in the wilderness. J. and R. were with me.
> (R. is often a figure of power in his dreams.) Some-
> thing dangerous was going to happen. I knew I could
> save them, but that a thousand years would pass be-
> fore we were safe. I first wondered if that were possi-
> ble, that I could live a thousand years. Then I knew
> I could. I told them to lie down. I planted my legs
> firmly on the ground, raised my arms to the sky, and
> yelled, "Let it begin." Everything suddenly became
> white with ice. The sky was a brilliant blue. The wind
> was blowing tremendously hard, but it couldn't move
> me. I was amazed at the colors, and enjoyed looking
> at them. Then I moved my arms to signal the end of
> the thousand years. The ice and blue left, and R.
> and J. stood up; they were safe. A thousand years had
> passed in ten or fifteen seconds.

He did not let his mental process of negative thinking (his
false clarity) stop the dream. "Let it begin" showed he was
taking more of a role, as he let feeling take over more and more
of his life. He was more aware of his feeling than he had been
in the first dream. This new dream had elements of power
dreaming showing that his feeling level and role were both
increasing. Indeed, in the first dream he was watching the
dream; in the second, the dreamer allowed the feeling to

occur. In this respect, luminous dreams frequently have elements in common with power dreams. Luminous dreams are important because they, more than others, lead to the transformative dream.

THE TRANSFORMATIVE DREAM

The dynamic of expression in dreaming ranges from dreams in which there is no obvious outward display of the dreamer's feelings or thoughts, to dreams in which the expression is so prolonged and complete that it dominates the dream. It is not necessary at this time to give an example of a dream without expression — the dream literature is full of them. The following dream is a good example of a dreamer expressing his feelings without restraint.

> I was walking somewhere outside and I saw my father. I don't remember whether I clearly knew I was dreaming, but I knew he was dead, or was dying, that I wouldn't see him anymore. (Patient's father had died that year.) I was sad for him, then for myself. I cried — the feeling was stronger the more I cried. I felt very sad that we didn't have more contact, that I had wanted to feel more with him than I had. Then I was very sad that I would die and all feeling would stop. I cried openly, deeply, and in my dream I couldn't see anything anymore. I was inside my body. My father's image disappeared, there was just my feeling, a deep sobbing feeling in my chest. That was the most deeply I have ever cried.

In this dream there is an obvious shift from images to feeling, from a symbolism of feeling to the reality of a deep body sensation. This dream contains elements of clarity and activity as well. The dream is transformative. The dreamer begins the dream walking somewhere with an image of his father, and ends with a deep sense of feeling inside his body, so deep that it extinguishes all images.

Whenever the dreamer carries out his role, expression, clarity, feeling, or contact to a great enough degree, there is often a shift in symbolism that is the hallmark of the transformative dream.[3] It is difficult to divide dreaming into specific types and kinds of dreams. There is overlap because the five dynamics we have been discussing exist to some extent in every dream. Further, it is impossible to change one dynamic within the dream without changing all of them. If the dreamer's role changes within the dream so that he becomes more active, then his feeling, clarity, expression, and contact are usually influenced as well. That is why we say dreaming is transformative.

The main characteristics of the transformative dream are full awareness, full role, full feeling, and full expression, plus a movement toward contact with other people. The power, clarity, and luminosity of other dreams are extended as the dreamer dramatically allows the dream to work and the symbolism to break down. The transformative dream is not an explosion; the dreamer is not loud or "cosmically conscious." Most transformative dreams are simple, strong, direct and realistic statements of the dreamer's feelings in the most complete picture possible. The statements are obvious and need no interpretation. Not only does the dreamer know what the dream is saying to him or her, but anyone who reads the dream has a related experience. The transformative dream is its own interpreter.

We have stated repeatedly that dreaming is transformative. For the normal dreamer all that is lacking is a waking life that does not disorder the feelings which are woven into dream pictures at night. As a patient's role, clarity, feeling, expression, and contact are brought into balance, his or her dreams reflect this new ordering process. The dynamics work for the affective drive at night, instead of against it, and are enhanced by the need to complete feelings in the dream.

The transformative dream can occur whenever the increase in dynamics is sufficient to begin to undo the dream symbols. Without the completeness we are talking about, the best the dreamer can do is to understand the dream through interpretation. Interpretation is outside the dream itself, and represents a structure imposed upon it.[4] Transformation occurs solely within the dream because the dream processes themselves are sufficient to undo the symbolism. The following represents a transformative dream. In it the dreamer relies heavily on an increase in feeling to undo the dream symbolism.

> *I was part of a very large road show. A traveling circus and theatrical company. I was walking through different tents and a big theater building. As I entered each room people were setting up for the shows. I recognized a lot of people, relatives and people from the seminary. They were all engrossed in their work. I was looking for something. I knew they were all lost in their work. In one tent some strangers were doing perverted things, like cutting someone open with scissors. I looked at them and said, "I'm leaving." I got to the door but it was locked and there was no door knob, only a hole. I took the scissors I had and put it in the hole and walked out. I was backstage now among the cables and props. I saw an old Jesuit friend who said we were supposed to serve mass at 4:30 P.M. I said, "You are late." I wanted to keep moving. People kept telling me things I had to do. I walked past them, through the curtains and into the open. It was not a stage. I was in front of the building. I could feel my chest fill with feeling—I began screaming out and throwing out my arms like a conqueror. "I'm really here," I yelled. "I'm really here." I knew I had walked into reality.*

Each picture in this dream represented a past association that had been interfering in his "real" life. This dream presented his past to him like the characters in a bizarre play, which was very much how his childhood and young adulthood had begun to seem to him. It was a tremendous new feeling that he experienced at the end. All the symbols were behind him, literally and figuratively.

The following dream is transformative. There is a shift which takes place due to an increase in dreamer role from being highly symbolic (the monster) to being less symbolic (the school book).

> I am in a swimming pool with C., my 9th grade friend.
> A monster is after him. I am afraid of monsters and
> I want C. to get hurt—but then when the monster
> starts on him, I attack and drown the monster which
> turns into a school book.

If there were subsequent expression of feeling based on the image of the school book, the dream would probably continue to unravel.

In the following example, the dreamer experiences elements of increased power, feeling, clarity, and role. The dream speaks for itself. It needs no introduction nor any interpretation to add to its completeness.

> I dreamt that I was over at my friend R.'s house. I
> was standing outside his front door, in the patio.
> Standing there was J., a patient of mine who was
> talking about quitting therapy. I told him that he
> shouldn't quit, that it was very hard, it was difficult
> to get to feelings, but that there was no other way
> other than to try very hard, not to give up. I told him
> that I had a three hour session that day, and the first
> two hours were spent by my therapist trying very hard
> to help me feel, trying everything that was necessary

*every minute. That I did everything he told me be-
cause I trusted him, and because I wanted to feel
better. After two hours I broke through my defenses
and felt deeply. There is no shortcut, no other way,
but through your friends who try and help, and the
faith in them and yourself, to try for yourself. I didn't
get sad, I didn't feel the urgency that I normally
feel trying to convince someone of anything. I felt the
same way I felt in the evening after the session—very
relaxed and open. As I talked to him I thought of
these things for the first time, and they were insights
to me, for I could feel how right they were, inside my
body, I felt myself change—I felt solid, firm, open
and soft and very heavy, all of these at the same time.*

The dreamer did have a patient who was talking to him that
day about stopping therapy. He lives across the street from his
friend in the dream, and had the therapy session he described
that previous afternoon. He went on to comment, "There was
nothing symbolic about the dream. I could feel myself in the
dream, and what I said to J., I took in for myself. It affected
me physically. I knew it was crucial for me to remember in
difficult times, when I feel bad and fantasize leaving or being
alone, the lessons of this dream. I was really talking clearly and
with feeling to myself."

We base our functional theory on dreams such as those we
have shown you. We consider this kind of dream not a super-
dream or even super-consciousness. We consider it an example
of a natural consciousness available to all who dream. We base
our theory and practice around the experience of transformative dreaming.

PRACTICAL ADVICE FOR USING DREAMS

If you want to apply the functional approach to your own dreams, you can now go beyond the three starter questions introduced at the end of Chapter 1. The functional analysis of dreams focuses on the way the dreamer is functioning and the way he or she could function. Specifically you can ask yourself, for any dream:

1. *"How expressive was I in this dream?"*

2. *"How active was I in this dream?"*

3. *"How clear was I in this dream?"*

4. *"How much feeling did I experience in this dream?"*

5. *"How much contact did I make with other people in this dream?"*

In the Appendix, we present detailed rating scales for a functional analysis of these dynamic characteristics but you can learn much about yourself and your dreams by simply asking these five general questions and making your own relative judgments. It is the activity of paying attention to these functional dynamics that is of importance, not how accurately you evaluate yourself.

4

FREUD: SYMBOLISM AND INTERPRETATION

Perhaps the greatest legacy of Sigmund Freud was not his theory of dreaming and his conceptualizations about psychopathology, but his personal search. Freud was trying to understand his own dreams and the secrets that he kept from himself. He studied his dreams and related them to life and so was able to advance dream theory. He formulated a theory and a method which allowed the sometimes confusing, bizarre and seemingly nonsensical expressions which occur in dreams to be deciphered into their hidden meanings about a dreamer's wishes and inner life.

Ancient dream theories[1] also ascribed hidden meanings to dreams but found these meanings *outside* the dreamer. Freud argued that dreams always told about the dreamer's life, either his present life or his childhood or both. His contribution fixed dream interpretation within the frame of reference of the dreamer's own life.

THE FULFILLMENT OF A WISH

Freud expressed the central idea of his theory in his first major work, *The Interpretation of Dreams*. Chapter three is simply titled "A Dream is the Fulfillment of a Wish." It is his succinct definition of a dream. Under it, all dreams become meaningful once we discover the hidden wishes that are disguised by the dream symbolism. Freud goes on to argue this in *New Intro-ductory Lectures:*

> What has been called the dream is the text of the dream or the *manifest* dream, and what we are look-ing for, what we suspect, so to say, of lying behind the dream, we shall describe as the *latent* dream thoughts. . . . We have to transform the manifest dream into the latent one, and to explain how, in the dreamer's mind the latter has become the former. (Freud, 1965, pp. 9-10)

Freud admits this dream explanation is incomplete since some transforming and explication are necessary to make the latent content apparent.

> The process by which the latent dream is transformed into the manifest dream is called the dream work; while the reverse process, which seeks to progress from the manifest to the latent thoughts, is our work of interpretation; the work of interpretation therefore aims at demolishing the dream work. (Freud, *A General Introduction to Psychoanalysis,* 1953, p. 179)

The discovery process, or interpretation, changes the dream from its symbolic form to its real form, and the wishes are dis-closed. A dream in its real form, according to Freud, has a clear *meaning.*

Freud used the following dream to illustrate his theory and method. It is often discussed in the literature as his "Irma Dream." He later related, "This is the first dream I submitted to a detailed interpretation." We can very clearly contrast our approach to working with dreams to the Freudians' by using this example of Freud's dream of July 23rd-24th, 1895.

> A large hall—numerous guests whom we were re-ceiving—among them was Irma. I at once took her on one side, as though to answer her letter and to

reproach her for not having accepted my "solution" yet. I said to her: "If you still get pains, it's really only your fault." She replied: "If you only knew what pains I've got now in my throat and stomach and abdomen." — I was alarmed and looked at her. She looked pale and puffy. I thought to myself that after all I must be missing some organic trouble. I took her to the window and looked down her throat and she showed signs of recalcitrance, like women with artificial dentures. I thought to myself that there was really no need for her to do that. She then opened her mouth properly and on the right I found a big white patch; at another place I saw extensive whitish grey scabs upon some remarkably curly structures which were evidently modeled on the turbinal bones of the nose. I at once called Dr. M., and he repeated the examination and confirmed it . . . Dr. M. looked quite different from usual; he was very pale, he walked with a limp and his skin was clean-shaven . . . My friend Otto was now standing beside her as well, and my friend Leopold was percussing her through her bodice and saying: "She has a dull area low down on the left." He also indicated that a portion of the skin on the left shoulder was infiltrated. (I noticed this, just as he did, in spite of her dress.) . . . M. said "There's no doubt it's an infection, but no matter, dysentery will supervene and the toxin will be eliminated." . . . We were directly aware, too, of the origin of the infection. Not long before, when she was feeling unwell, my friend Otto had given her an injection of propyl, propyls . . . propionic acid . . . trimethylthylamin (and I saw before me the formula for this printed in heavy type) . . . Injections of that sort ought not to be made so thoughtlessly . . . And probably the syringe had not been clean. (Freud, *The Interpretation of Dreams,* 1960, p. 107)

Freud proceeds to analyze the dream by first recounting the events of the previous day which were partially represented in his dream, and then by giving his associations to each of the elements of the dream. For example, his mention of the final image of the dream is as follows:

> *And probably the syringe had not been clean.* This was yet another accusation against Otto, but derived from a different source. I had happened the day before to meet the son of an old lady of eighty-two to whom I had given an injection of morphine twice a day. At the moment she was in the country and was suffering from phlebitis. I had at once thought it must be an infiltration caused by a dirty syringe. I was proud of the fact that in two years I had not caused a single infiltration . . . (Freud, 1960, p. 118)

He concluded his interpretation with this summary:

> The dream fulfilled certain wishes which were stunted in me by the events of the previous evening (the news given me by Otto and my writing out of the case history). The conclusion of the dream, that is to say, was that I was not responsible for the persistence of Irma's pains, but that Otto was. Otto had in fact annoyed me by his remarks about Irma's incomplete cure and the dream gave me my revenge by throwing the reproach back on to him. The dream acquitted me for the responsibility of Irma's condition by show-ing that it was due to other factors — it produced a whole series of reasons. The dream represented a particular state of affairs as I should have wished it to be. *Thus its content was the fulfillment of a wish and its motive was a wish.* (Freud, 1960, pp. 114-15)

Freud intended this dream and its interpretation to show that dreams are wish fulfillments, not necessarily to demonstrate the dynamics of his theories in action. But this example also encompasses the fundamental way Freud saw dreams—as symbolic messages about wish-messages. The dream ends with an understanding. This understanding is a substitute for expressing feeling. He continues to dream in the same symbolic way, and to translate the message over and over, like constantly repairing and adjusting something broken. We never find out if Freud would feel better using another approach.

To use another approach would be to make an active choice. It implies change. Interpretation can become passive when we are left solely with insights, as in this dream. If "wishes were stunted by the events of the previous day," then events control expression. If we play this type of role, we are not free to take responsibility for our own experience. The dream seen as wish fulfillment is an ending to a sentence, a closed message. The dream seen as a feeling trying for completion is a beginning, an opening to more feeling, and more action.

We believe psychological theories should not only explain but educate. This is a controversial position. Some people think that psychological theories perform the same function as physical or biological theories. They do not because objects are not affected by the theories we have about them, and people are. Freud's theory does not push the dreamer towards change, it explains him. Functional dream theory focuses on changing the dreamer.

Freud's Irma dream has a different message for us. Assuming that the feelings revealed in the dream parallel those of his waking state, we would encourage the patient, Sigmund, within a therapy session, to express directly the things he had felt but not said to Otto, such as, "I don't like what you said," or "Don't talk to me that way." We would not stop with Freud's understanding of his feelings but move toward a full expression of feeling. His "annoyance" might turn to anger and his "responsibility" could become sadness. By experiencing his feelings he would make the first step toward transformation — to begin to match his inner feelings with his outer expression of those feelings. If he could do this within the therapy session and continue to express himself more fully beyond the session, we would expect that, eventually, Freud's dreams would begin to change; he would occasionally dream transformatively. He would shift from symbolic, censored and indirect expression of feeling to more direct expression within his dream.

FREUD'S PUNISHMENT DREAM

Freud's attempts to explain all dreams as compensations or wish fulfillments fit least well those dreams in which the dreamer is undergoing something unpleasant. The most common form of such dreams is one in which the dreamer is haunted by unpleasant memories from his past. Freud calls these dreams "punishment dreams" and offers two explanations for their occurrence. First, he says, these dreams result from "masochistical impulses of the mind." They satisfy the unconscious wishes of the ego that "the dreamer may be punished for a repressed and forbidden wishful impulse" (Freud, 1960, pp. 513, 596). A wish to be punished for a wish! The second explanation is based on the Freudian structural conception of ego, id and super-ego forces. Punishment dreams satisfy the wishes of the essentially punitive part of the personality, the conscience or super-ego. A wish to punish!

Freud cites a "punishment dream" reported by the Austrian writer Peter Rosegger. Early in his life Rosegger had been a poor journeyman tailor. In his recurrent dream he would find himself, once again, back in the unpleasant milieu of the tailor's shop.

> I knew well enough, as I sat like that beside him (master), sewing and ironing, that my right place

was no longer there and that as a townsman I had
other things to occupy me. But I was always on vaca-
tion, I was always having holidays, and so it was that
I sat beside my master as his assistant. It often irked
me and I felt sad at the loss of time in which I might
well have found better and more useful things to do.
Now and then, when something went awry, I had to
put up with a scolding from my master, though there
was never any talk of wages. Often, as I sat there with
bent back in the dark workshop, I thought of giving
notice and taking my leave. Once I even did so; but
my master paid me no heed and I was seen sitting
beside him again and sewing . . . The most reasonable thing to do, I thought, would be to stand up
and tell him that I was only with him to please him
and then go off. But I did not do so. I made no objection when my master took on an apprentice and
ordered me to make room for him on the bench. I
moved into the corner and sewed. (Freud, 1960, pp.
473-74)

In the dream, Rosegger was finally dismissed by the master
and, in his words, "my fright at this was so overpowering that
I awoke." It is not clear in this example that the dreamer is
punishing himself. What seems obvious, however, is that
Rosegger never completely expressed the feelings he had toward the tailor who frightened him and abused him. The
impulses to express anger are clearly evident, but the expression
does not occur. We would speculate that this dream recurs
because Rosegger is still not able to express certain feelings,
such as anger, but continuously relives his past. If he were
helped to feel how he defends against the expression of anger
in the present, and how these defenses were generated in his
past, he would be able to begin to choose new ways of expression in his waking life. It would then be possible for him to

begin to dream more actively and expressively. He might even have the following dream:

> . . . *And then I said to him, "You're not my master any longer. Get away from me." I then kicked and pushed him out the door and the tailor shop became my study. I felt relief and strength. I knew I could begin to show my anger. My fear came from being silent and sitting there.*

Freud's basic thesis is that dreams are wish fulfillments. But wishes are feelings that have not been fully expressed. The wish fulfillment theory takes dreams as fixed messages, not as mutable forms of expression. It thus bypasses the dynamic shift from passive, incomplete, symbolic non-expression to active, complete, and direct expression. Neither the theory nor the dream which illustrates it allows for movement toward expression and nonsymbolism.

An extremely interesting personal account of the benefits and limits of the psychoanalytic interpretive approach to dreams is now available in Dr. Abraham Kardiner's book *My Analysis with Freud* (1977). Kardiner reports a pivotal dream in the analysis which Freud subtly and accurately interpreted, concluding with ". . . [you] remained submissive and obedient to him in order not to arouse the sleeping dragon, the angry father." Kardiner comments:

> My immediate reaction was to accept Freud's interpretation. It was not until many years later that I understood the basic error committed here by Freud. The man who had invented the concept of transference did not recognize it when it occurred here. He overlooked one thing: *Yes, I was afraid of my father in childhood, but the one whom I feared now was Freud himself.* He could make me or break me which my father no longer could. By his statement he

pushed the entire reaction into the past, thereby making the analysis an historical reconstruction (Kardiner, 1977, p. 58)

Such a therapeutic error would be less likely to occur within the functional approach to dreams because we would focus on *how* the dreamer functioned in his dream and in his life, not on what caused the dream. Of course we can, within the functional approach, also look for the sources of arrested functioning but we would do so not merely to trace the cause, but to return the patient to transformative functioning. To do that, the patient needs to express his real feelings in the present, to the therapist and others in his life.

Our basic thesis is that dreams are attempts to complete feelings which were left incomplete. Obviously this agrees with Freud's thesis to the extent that wishes are incomplete feelings. But the transformation theory includes but does not limit itself to the wish fulfillment theory. Our theory is more general than Freud's.

SYMBOLISM, INTERPRETATION AND TRANSFORMATION

There is an often told story about a man who tells his analyst, "Last night I had this dream about keys and locks." The analyst interprets the dream for the patient, to show him that he was symbolically dreaming about sexual intercourse. So the next day he reports another dream, this time about having sex with his wife, and he quickly adds, "But I know I was really dreaming about keys and locks." While this well-worn clinical joke oversimplifies both what analysts do and what dreamers report, it poses several important questions about dreams. First, what is the function of dreaming—what does dreaming about locks and keys accomplish for the dreamer *while* dreaming? Second, when is a dream symbolic, and when is it real or directly representational—when are we dreaming about sex, and when about locks and keys? Third, where do symbols originate? Are they mysterious products of an unknown night-time physiological mechanism, or are they derived from the dreamer's daytime experience? Fourth, do nonsymbolic dreams occur? And fifth, if they do occur, is it possible to shift from symbolic to nonsymbolic dreaming *within* a dream? Can dreams become nonsymbolic without outside interpretation?

In fairness, we should say that Freud's answers to these questions are limited because they are not his questions. However, part of the task of advancing a research area is to give new answers to old questions; the other is to ask new questions. Freud did this himself when he asked, "Can nonsensical dreams be interpreted to make sense?" We accept some of Freud's answers to his questions, and more importantly, we recognize that his questions, and the volumes of clinical work that have accumulated around Freudian dream theory, provide us with a body of knowledge from which we can make advances.

WHAT IS THE FUNCTION OF DREAMING?

Freud argues that during sleep, dreams do what has not been done in waking—dreams have a compensatory function. His answer to this question has often been shortened: dreams protect sleep. But his fuller answer is more significant and more general.

> Dreaming has taken on the task of bringing back under control of the preconscious the excitation in the unconscious which has been left free; in so doing it discharges the unconscious excitation, serves it as a safety valve and at the same time preserves the sleep of the preconscious in return for a small expenditure of waking activity. (Freud, 1960, p. 579)

Freud believes dreams compensate for unresolved excitation in the unconscious, making it conscious in a new form. Since this new form exists at a lower level of excitement it allows sleep to continue. Although some energy, such as tossing and turning, murmuring, or movement, is utilized in return for this compensation, it is small in comparison to the amount of energy that is discharged through this "safety valve." Dreams not only protect sleep, they protect waking as well. According to Freud, we don't have to start the next day with an over-loaded unconscious.

We believe that dreaming is a natural releasing activity in which feelings that were not expressed or not fully expressed during the day try to come to completion through expression. Symbolic dreams give a partial release while transformative dreams move toward a full release. Dreaming is expressive as well as compensatory.

Dreaming is not the "guardian of sleep" but the agent of feeling. Sleep does not need protection. This is too confining a concept. We can have as much and sometimes more excitement and feeling at night as we have during the day. Once we shift into the transformative mode of dreaming, nighttime experiences become "vehicles of expression" which can move the dreamer into places and times not yet visited in waking. Dreaming becomes a powerful experience, sometimes prospective in feeling *and* meaning.[2]

WHEN ARE DREAMS SYMBOLIC?

Except for children's dreams and very trivial and infrequent adult dreams, Freud would say that dreams are always symbolic because the dream work mechanism, or censor, is always converting direct wishes into indirect symbols. He says there are no innocent dreams—dreams that are directly expressive. "What we dream is either manifestly recognizable as psychically significant (rare or nonexistent), or it is distorted and cannot be judged until the dream has been interpreted (the usual case). Dreams need interpretation to become complete" (Freud, 1960, p. 182).

We disagree. Dreams are symbolic when the dreamer has not completed his or her feelings during waking life; they are nonsymbolic when the feelings have been completed. Transformative or nonsymbolic dreams, far from being trivial or innocent, are the best indicators that a person is living his or her feelings.

WHERE DO SYMBOLS ORIGINATE?

Although Freud clearly describes such dream work mechanisms as displacement, condensation, and secondary revision, he never really explains where these mechanisms of distortion originate or whether dream work is an eternally existing and healthy part of our neurophysiology or not. Symbols arise from two sources. First, they are the result of the translation of words, perceptions, and actions in waking life, to the pictures or images of dreaming. Freud treats this aspect adequately. Secondly, they result from the disordering or mixing of feeling components that occurs when feelings are not completed. Here Freud is vague; we are never sure whether he believes the dream work mechanism is pathologically acquired. We believe it is. Feeling disorders are not caused by dream censors, or dream work mechanisms intrinsic to the dreamer. The mechanisms are caused by the external disordering that children and adults undergo. These mechanisms of disordering or distortion (such as substitution) are learned. Dreaming is naturally distortion-free.

Children have more intense dreams than adults, and more nightmares, because they have more intense feelings during the day. At the beginning stages of disordering they are unable to symbolize enough of their feelings left incomplete during the day to avoid experiencing them at night.[3] As adults, our symbolization has both a present cause, the way we disordered our expression during the day, and an antecedent from the past.

CAN DREAMS BE NONSYMBOLIC?

Freud recognizes that nonsymbolic dreams can occur, but his evaluation of their significance is limited to using them as proof for his theory of dreams as wish fulfillments.

> The dreams of young children are frequently pure wish-fulfillments and are in that case quite uninteresting compared with the dreams of adults. They raise no problems for solution, but on the other hand are of inestimable importance in proving that, in their essential nature, dreams represent fulfillments of wishes. (Freud, 1960, p. 125)

We feel nonsymbolic dreams imply something far more significant. If disorder can lead to progressively more symbolization, then conversely, reordering or transformative living leads to progressively less symbolization in dreaming. The movement toward complete expression of feelings in waking leads to transformative dreaming. Transformative dreaming occurs in two ways. First, there is an increase in nonsymbolic dreaming. Second, there is a shift within a dream, from symbolic to direct nonsymbolic expression. The following are examples of the kinds of dream that occur with increasing frequency and illustrate the first type of nonsymbolic dreaming.

> *I am talking to N. (wife). She and I are fighting and I feel myself going away from her and me. I stop fighting and say to myself, "I want." She has to feel how she feels—I want. And then I feel my own body. I feel I want (dreamer's emphasis).*

Although the dream does not represent a complete expression, such as verbalizing "I want," it does present a shift in awareness and clarity from symbolism (fighting) to real feeling (wanting).

In the following, a therapist dreams about a patient of his who lived next door, and was not living honestly from his feelings.

> *Me telling R., "You have to be more honest in your daily life and make a commitment to this therapy."*

This dream in itself is not remarkable, but placed in the context of a dreamer who is gradually changing the way he or she dreams from being symbolic to being directly expressive, it achieves its importance.

The second type contains a shift from the normal symbolism usually found in dreams, to direct expression. Freud gave no indication that he was acquainted with this type of dream at all. We gave an example of this type of dream in the prototypic transformative dream on page three.

CAN SYMBOLIC TO NONSYMBOLIC SHIFTS OCCUR WITHIN A DREAM?

Freud does not recognize the possibility of shifts from symbolic to nonsymbolic dreaming within a dream. In his view dream censorship is not overcome except indirectly, through the postdream counterwork of interpretation. He would say that once the dream work mechanism is engaged, it stays engaged. We posit overcoming the dream work mechanism as the goal of dream transformation. Without this goal in mind, therapeutic work with dreams becomes bogged down in the hunt for the meaning of symbols. In actuality this disengagement can be striking and the hunt quite short.

> *I am being chased by a gorilla. He is very large and menacing. I run away. Finally I realize I must face him or keep running away. As I stop and face him he turns into a man who tells me—I must be more specific when talking about my feelings.*

By facing increasing feeling in the form of the monster symbol, he transforms the symbol. A similar transformation also occurs in the following dream.

> *I dreamt I was in a scary unknown house with many scary creatures. I have finally begun to open doors and fight my way through the rooms—the house changed into the house in which I used to live in Phoenix.*

In the following transformative dream, the dreamer had just returned from a week-long visit with his family. In a therapy session upon his return, he talked about how he had expressed more than he had any previous visit, but that he did "put up with things I really didn't need to . . . I had acted like I did as a child." In the dream he had after the session, he noted that he "acted the way I really am now."

> *In kitchen with parents. Mother wants to talk to M. (my brother). She says quietly, "M . . . M." Then she shouts, "M.!M.!" very angrily. She starts to leave. I am aware of no particular feeling. Then I begin to get angry. I see my father stabbing M. in the shoulders for answering my mother angrily. I begin to yell at them, and as I yell, I realize they have no sense at all hurting my brother. He wasn't doing anything wrong. I realize they are like children and I am an adult. I can really feel my anger all through my body. I enjoy the powerful feeling. My parents run away and stay at a distance, outside the kitchen.*

In citing examples of this type of transformative dream, we are applying the Maslowian strategy[4] of seeking the exceptional "good case." This strategy of seeking the exceptional gives us a perspective on normal (symbolic) dreams. Normal dreams follow the usual disordered pattern; they are not the optimal mode of dream life. We see exciting new possibilities in our observations of transformative dreams and they form the essence of our disagreement with Freud. Since we argue that transformative dreams are natural, and what are usually called adult dreams are pathological, we are also led to a very optimistic view of daytime behavior—one which is less symbolic and more real.

Our new theory of dreams gives answers that are sometimes slightly different and sometimes very different from those given by Freud. Freud's major concern is with the interpretation of dreams; we are concerned with the transformation of dreams. Freud states that "when the work of interpretation has been completed, we perceive that a dream is the fulfillment of a wish" (Freud, 1960, p. 121). We say that when the work of transformation is completed, the dreamer feels that what was left incomplete in the dream—the partial feeling—is made complete. Rather than compensate, dreams complete feelings.

In our orientation, a dream's real form is its feeling (sensation, meaning and expression). By stressing that dreams are personal messages, Freud implies that the dream pictures stand for words. Since Freud, much effort has been spent looking for a dream language, so that the dream experiences could be translated and compared. In the functional approach, we regard dreams as pictures of the way the dreamer deals with his feelings. We are no more concerned with language during the night than we are during the day. *How* a person talks is more revealing than *what* he says. In dreaming, *how* a person dreams (expresses, moves, feels) is more important than *what* he actually dreams (language, symbols). This change of emphasis creates a new direction for dream research, away from content analysis, toward process evaluation[5] of emotional functioning.

Freud made much of the distinction between latent content and manifest content. Our own emphasis is different. We stress not differences between hidden and visible *contents,* but the functional differences between expressed feelings and withheld feelings. It is our contention that this is a more valuable emphasis for two reasons. First, the difference between latent and manifest content is produced from feelings that are withheld. Second, concern with function leads to an emphasis on movement from defensiveness to expressiveness while concern with content stops with insight. No amount of interpretive insight will bring about a transformative shift from symbolic low-level functioning to expressiveness.

Both dream interpretation, or understanding a dream, and dream transformation, expressing feelings in a dream, can be complementary. However, transformation supercedes interpretation.[6] It is not possible to transform a dream without also understanding it, but it is easily possible to understand a dream without feeling it, or changing the dream from being a symbolic feeling *representation* to a nonsymbolic feeling *expression*. In fact, if someone becomes so focused on understanding his dream life or his waking life that he does not feel himself, and change the way he lives, then interpretation has become a defensive activity. Concern with content can stop expressive movement while concern with process emphasizes movement.

5

OTHER DREAM THEORISTS: JUNG, PERLS, AND BOSS

An unspeakable horror seized me. There was a darkness; then a dizzy, sickening sensation of sight that was not like seeing: I saw a Line that was no Line; Space that was not Space: I was myself, and not myself. When I could find voice, I shrieked aloud in agony, "Either this is madness or it is Hell." "It is neither," calmly replied the voice of the Sphere, "it is Knowledge; it is Three Dimensions: open your eye once again and try to look steadily."

(E.A. Abbott, *Flatland*, 1884)

Over ninety years ago, E.A. Abbott, in his book *Flatland*, described the problems inherent in creating awareness of greater dimensions within ourselves. His characters—lines, points, squares and spheres—all had to overcome tremendous inertia to increase their visions beyond what they thought was possible. Abbott made the simple, but important point, that you cannot experience yourself and your world fully, without moving from *here* to *there;* that you need some perspective in order to feel what you are doing in your life.

In the simplest terms, every therapy and every dream theory is concerned with getting from here to there: from problems to solutions, from confusion to clarity, from neurosis to normal, from less feeling to more feeling. All therapies and theories promise some movement from *here* to *there*. They differ in ways they attempt to undertake the journey, and in their vision of a destination. In this chapter, we will investigate this second factor, and see how it intricately influences the first. We will see that "vision affects method."

Jung, Perls and Boss shared with Freud the implicit belief that the dream may be valuable in providing the vision necessary for movement. Freud moved *here* and *back,* Jung moved *here* and *out* into the realm of transpersonal consciousness, Perls tried to move from *here* to *more here,* into the realm of personal affect, while Boss stressed the importance of the dream as its own experience, *simply here.* In this chapter we will further elaborate our transformative theory by comparing our vision with those of Jung, Perls and Boss; our dreams with their dreams; and finally, our theory with theirs. We will see how their work and their vision connects to our own functional theory of dreams and dream transformation.

JUNG'S VISION FORWARD

> For many years I have carefully analyzed about a thousand dreams per annum [and have] thus . . . acquired a certain experience in this matter. (Jung, *Dreams,* 1974, p. v)

Jung's vast experience with his own dreams and the dreams of his patients led him to formulations that went in directions different from those taken by Freud. We can best understand their differences by starting with the ideas they shared. Both Freud and Jung start from the idea that a dream is occasioned by emotional influences during the day which are then constellated by "complexes" from the past.

> Every emotion produces a more or less extensive complex of associations which I have called the "feel-

ing-toned complex of ideas" . . . The complexes appear as the chief components of the psychological disposition in every psychic structure. In the dream, for example, we encounter the emotional components, for it is easy to understand that all the products of psychic activity depend above all upon the strongest "constellating" influences. (Jung, 1974, p. 4)

Freud sought to identify and resolve the complexes hidden in dream symbols by getting from here (the dream) *back* to causal conditions in the patient's near and distant past which produced the complex. Jung, in contrast, tried to use the dream symbols to go from here (the dream) *forward,* to teach the dreamer how he or she might progress from his or her complexes to resolutions of them in the future.

Considering a dream from the standpoint of finality which I contrast with the causal standpoint of Freud, does not . . . involve a denial of the dream's causes, but rather a different interpretation of the associative material gathered round the dream . . . The question may be formulated simply as follows: What is the purpose of this dream? What effect is it meant to have? (Jung, 1974, p. 29)

. . . Freud's view that dreams have an essentially wish-fulfilling and sleep-preserving function is too narrow, even though the basic thought of a compensatory biological function is certainly correct . . . Dreams, I maintain, are compensatory to the conscious situation of the moment . . . A compensatory content is especially intense when it has vital significance for conscious orientation. (Jung, 1974, p. 40)

Jung was interested in the consequences or the future of the dream. It was a broadening shift from cause to effect. This broadening of Freud's work is clearly similar to the shift we described between Freud's wish fulfillment principle and our enlarged completion principle. Jung then adds another important broadening:

> I should like to distinguish between the *prospective* function of dreams and their *compensatory* function. The latter means that the unconscious, considered as relative to consciousness, adds to the conscious situation all those elements from the previous day which remained subliminal because of repression or because they were simply too feeble to reach consciousness . . . The prospective function on the other hand, is an anticipation in the unconscious of future conscious achievements, something like a preliminary exercise or sketch . . . Its symbolic content sometimes outlines the solution of a conflict . . . (Jung, 1974, p. 41)

To interpret the prospective meaning of a dream, Jung devised techniques which included, but went beyond, the association methods devised by Freud. In "amplification" the dream and the analyst consult historical and other outside sources to trace the meanings of symbols. "Active imagination" involves encouraging the patient to continue the dream in waking. The dreamer continues in his imagination the conservations and events of the dream, in effect completing the plot. Finally, he employed the "dream series method" in which the dream is related to the dreams which precede it and follow it, to see if there is a dream-to-dream development of symbols.

Jung justifies these methods by theoretically distinguishing between the personal and the collective unconscious:

> Thus we speak on the one hand of a personal and on the other of a *collective* unconscious, which lies at a deeper level and is further removed from conscious-

ness than personal unconscious. The "big" or "meaningful" dreams come from this deeper level . . . Such
dreams occur mostly during the critical phases of life,
in early youth, puberty, at the onset of middle age
(thirty-six to forty), and within sight of death . . .
these archetypal products are no longer concerned
with personal experiences but with general ideas,
whose chief significance lies in their intrinsic meaning
and not in any personal experience and its associations. (Jung, 1974, p. 77)

If there is a transpersonal, collective unconscious, then the
method of amplification is justified since the images within a
dream are not the exclusive property of the dreamer, but are
instead a common human heritage. Jung applied the methods
of active imagination and amplification to both personal
dreams and archetypal dreams, but they are of special value,
he asserts, in working with the latter.

Here Jung has made a significant departure from Freud,
and greatly enlarges Freud's vision. Freud based his psychoanalytic theory on the normal or wish-fulfilling dream. Jung
expanded Freudian dream theory right here by using a bigger
dream as a model, a dream with prospective significance. This
vision could allow for more movement than the normal dream;
from here to there could be extended by the very power and
beauty of the archetypal dream. This could happen, but it
doesn't. Jung weakens the prospective power of the dream for
the dreamer by stating that this greater dream has less personal
significance. At the last second he replaced a vision and possible movement with history and interpretation. He retained his
Freudian roots.

JUNG'S THEORY AND OUR THEORY
Our own theory is both in agreement and at odds with Jung's.
We agree that dreams are more than wish-fulfillment compen-

sations. But Jung only alludes to the possibility that they are attempts to complete what has been left incomplete in waking; he does this by asking for the effect of the dream. This difference in emphasis is crucial—it is the difference between a suggestion and a theory. We also agree that dreams are prospective as well as retrospective, that they frequently indicate directions of action and feeling a dreamer needs to take in his life. We disagree about the function and source of archetypal dreams and, more importantly, we believe that *archetypal or big dreams can only show their complete significance when followed by transformative dreams.* By seeing the function and source of archetypal dreams rooted in an impersonal past, Jung was prevented from looking for and finding a dream as intensely personal and powerful as the transformative dream.

We also agree with Jung that it is useful to examine a dream as a part of a dream series although we look for different changes than he did. He placed his vision on a transpersonal level. The dreams in series then become increasingly less personal and more general. In the transformational framework, the dreams between here (normal dreaming) and there (transformative dreaming) become increasingly personal and specific.

We would agree with Jung that archetypal or big dreams occur at times when there is a critical need for more consciousness, or in our language, when there is a need for a shift from one level of feeling to an expanded level. Again, his vision involves an expanded range of feeling *within* the person. The critical question becomes: Does the shift occur? Does transformation take place?

In order to answer the last question, we quote one dream from a dream series of 400 dreams which Jung analyzed. He used the method of amplification to bring out the collective meanings of the dream.

In a primeval forest. An elephant looms up menacingly. Then a large ape-man, bear, or cave man threatens to attack the dreamer with a club. Suddenly the man with the painted beard appears and stares at the aggressor, so that he is spellbound. But the dreamer is terrified. The voice says, "Everything must be ruled by the light." (Jung, 1974, Dream 22, p. 163)

Jung refers to a 15th century medieval painting of a wild man and comments:

... friend "painted beard" appears in the scene as an obliging *deus ex machina* and exorcises the annihilation threatened by the formidable ape-man ... The voice finally declares, "Everything must be ruled by the light," which presumably means the light of the discerning, conscious mind, a genuine *illumination* honestly acquired ... With the active intervention of the intellect a new phase of the unconscious process begins: the conscious mind must now come to terms with the figures of the unknown woman ("anima"), the unknown man ("the shadow"), the wise old man ("mana personality"), and the symbols of the self. (Jung, 1974, pp. 166–67)

Jung argues that transformation, which he calls "individuation," is indicated when there is *progression in the symbols*. The patient who had this last dream eventually dreamt in more and more abstract images until finally his dreams came to resemble "mandalas." In our view this progression actually represents a *failure* of transformation. Only if a big dream is eventually *followed* by a transformative dream has a significant shift occurred in the patient's life.

We believe transformation is indicated when there is a *progression in feeling expression*. There must be an increase in the functional dynamics (the dreamer's emotional characteristics). Without such an increase, and without an eventual shift from symbolism to realism, the dreams and the dreamer remain abstract and unworldly.

In this case, the movement from "here to there" is going in the wrong direction. For Jung the direction is toward mandalas and for us it is toward nonsymbolic dreaming. The key to understanding where this difference begins is our contention that Jung's big dream must be followed by an even bigger dream, the transformative dream, or at least a power dream, to indicate that a feeling shift has occurred in the patient's personal dynamics. In all fairness to Jung, the necessary requirements in the patient's life were not met, and he was unable to maintain the level of feeling or do what the dream told him. The patient approached and then receded from transformation.

We would consider Jung's sample dream transformative if the dreamer had personalized his or her experience so that there would be more feeling derived from the dreamer's own expressive action. We would expect to see a shift in the setting from an unfamiliar one that lets the dreamer have feeling *about* (the primeval forest), to a familiar one from his or her own present or past. Secondly, we might expect to see a similar shift in the character images. The elephant, cave man, or man with the painted beard could become recognized as actual figures from the dreamer's life. Finally, the abstract admonition, "Everything must be ruled by the light," could take on greater significance if he himself said "I need to be more clear about how I feel." This shift may seem to substitute the extramundane for the mundane. But the intensification of feeling brought about by such a transformation would be anything but dull—it would be a revivification of the dreamer's waking and dreaming life.

From this we can see how Jung built on his Freudian foundation and carried us at least one step further, one dimension deeper into our own feeling awareness of ourselves. He stopped the vision at this point and began to look back, not forward; retrospectively, not prospectively. Rather than working with the expanded feeling associated with the images in the archetypal dream and living the resultant signficance, he brought in more classical Freudian interpretations from the past, and extended them to include even more than the patient's personal history.[1]

THE VALUE OF SYMBOLS

People who have heard us lecture about the functional approach to dreaming and transformative dreams sometimes falsely conclude that we are saying symbolism is unnecessary and harmful. They summarize our arguments with the oversimplification—"all symbolic dreams are bad; all nonsymbolic dreams are good." We are definitely not making such a statement.

The primary emphasis in the functional approach is on recognizing and changing the emotional traits of the dreamer, the shift from symbolism to realism is a secondary emphasis, but there is a correlation—more effective emotional functioning eventually leads to more realistic dreams.

However, it is very often the case that more symbolism is the next step towards less symbolism. One of the great values of symbolic dreams is that they show, in pictures, how absurd seemingly rational, habitual images of oneself can be. For example, an image of "I can't show anything" might be represented with the dreamer being attacked by his enemies while his friends are all around him. Perhaps only one word would be necessary to save him, and he is frustrated because he is unable to make a sound. This type of dream often has a great impact on the dreamer. It gives the dreamer an experience of the restricting consequences of an image on one's body and one's life.

Another value of increased symbolism is shown in what

Jung referred to as numinous images. A numinous image is one of almost mystic power reflecting increased general feeling that allows the dreamer to have a fresh perspective on his or her life. It symbolizes a direction for the dreamer to pursue in waking which will lead to transformation.

The value of such symbolic or numinous dreams is very great. Movement from one level of feeling to another is not accomplished with one simple expression of feeling. To integrate one's life at a more sensitive and expressive feeling level requires weeks, months, and years. We often observe that the consequences of a simple therapeutic session may take many months to "live out." It is the same for dreams. The numinous dream provides a symbol for the dreamer's new way of living. The symbol functions to help the dreamer remember how he or she can be. A powerful symbol is required to overcome the inertia of old habits of non-feeling. Therefore, far from always being bad, a symbol or image that works for the dreamer, rather than against him or her, can counter the inertia of forgetfulness.

Forgetfulness is the enemy of effective emotional functioning and consciousness. Psychotherapists have made numerous observations about the processes of repression but none have commented on the process of forgetfulness. Repression occurs when a person unconsciously does not complete feelings and withholds them in ways that were learned in the past. The process of forgetfulness occurs when a person moves away from that new expressiveness back into an image from which he or she had already escaped. Once a feeling block is made conscious and the potentiality for new expressiveness is available, the new feeling possibilities may still not be followed. Instead of making a conscious choice based on one's own experience — remembering — the person chooses to pretend unconsciousness.

One of the special values of working with dreams in psychotherapy and in dream communities is that the effort to remember and use dreams is a direct counter to forgetfulness. Everyone is familiar with the early morning inertia that works against paying attention to dreams and writing them down. Giving in to that particular kind of dream non-remembering or forgetfulness is exactly the same, experientially, as forgetting to respond in new ways. When you remember your dreams, you start the day with an alertness or awareness that works against forgetfulness.

The dream practitioner who, after Jung, most concerned himself with realizing and making conscious this moment-by-moment import of dreams was Fritz Perls. Rather than expanding the significance of the dream into the dreamer's future or past, into causal or effectual relevancies, he pushed the dream into the realm of present affect.

PERLS' METHODS OF WORKING WITH DREAMS

There is a direct but usually unrecognized connection between Jung and Perls.[2] Essentially, Perls adopted Jung's active methods of working with dreams, but applied them within a Freudian orientation toward the unconscious. He worked with *personal* rather than impersonal complexes, but explored their "here and now" meaning in the person's life rather than delving back for a causal meaning. Jung says:

> The whole dream work is essentially subjective and a dream is a theatre in which the dreamer is himself the scene, the player, the prompter, the producer, the author, the public and the critic. This simple truth forms the basis for a conception of the dream's meaning which I have called *interpretation on the subjective level.* Such an interpretation, as the term implies, conceives all the figures in the dream as per-

sonified features of the dreamer's own personality.
(Jung, 1974, p. 52)

This is the same thing that Perls says:

> . . . I suggest you write the dream down and make a
> list of *all* the details in the dream. Get every person,
> every thing, every mood, and then work on these to
> *become* each one of them. Ham it up, and really
> transform yourself into each of the different items
> . . . Next, take each one of these different items,
> characters, and parts and let them have encounters
> between them. Write a script . . . have a dialogue
> between the opposing parts and you will find — espe-
> cially if you get the correct opposites — that they
> always start out fighting each other. All the differ-
> ent parts — any part in the dream is yourself, is a
> projection of yourself . . . (Perls, *Gestalt Therapy
> Verbatim,* 1969, p. 69)

Both Jung and Perls regard dream symbols as complexes
personified in dreams and both apply methods of active expression to bring out the meanings and feelings associated with
these complexes. Jung's images get bigger and bigger to contain the feelings that are tapped through imaginative contact
with feeling-laden images. Perls, by contrast, attempts to dis-
solve or burst the image by having it acted out. In 1936 Fritz
Perls gave a paper at the International Psychoanalytic Congress in Czechoslovakia (Perls, *In and Out the Garbage Pail,*
1969). He reported complete disapproval because the analysts
in attendance at the Congress were stuck on content interpretations. He tried to arrive at feeling resolutions behind contra-
dictory images by giving each conflicting image in the dream
full expression.

Perls' results, but not his methods, are much closer to the
functional way of working with dreams.

> . . . a dream is condensed reflection of our existence.
> What we don't realize enough is that we devote our
> lives to a dream: a dream of glory, usefulness, do-
> gooder, gangster, or whatever we dream of. And in
> many people's lives, through self-frustration, our
> dream turns into a nightmare . . . When we come to
> our senses, we start to *see*, to *feel,* to experience our
> needs and satisfactions instead of playing roles and
> needing such a lot of props . . . (Perls, 1969, p. 177)

In this passage Perls begins to state something very close to
one of our beliefs — dreams are the way they are because waking is the way it is. But when he alludes to changes when awake,
he does not mention a corresponding change in dream process.
We do not know what will happen when "we come to our
senses, we start to see, to feel" in our dreams. There is no
"gestalt dream" that could unify the parts of ourselves that
come to life in the dream. Returning again and again to the
dream itself, Perls had to rely on method or technique at the
expense of his vision. He realized, though, that from "here to
there" meant a journey to deeper levels of feeling, even if his
vision was so fixed on the dreams he was analyzing that he did
not see where that journey would lead.

THE DIFFERENCES BETWEEN OUR METHOD AND
PERLS' METHOD

Having stated these alignments and disagreements in theory,
we must hasten to show the differences between our methods
of working with dreams, and those developed by Perls. We do
not regularly employ dream dialogue techniques or psycho-
dramas to get dreamers to act out elements of their dreams.
These methods, although useful if applied infrequently in
specific and limited instances, are basically misleading if over-
used. They become gimmicks. Perls himself was well aware of
the dangers of this overuse:

A technique is a gimmick. A gimmick should only be used in an extreme case . . . These techniques, these tools, are quite useful in some seminar on sensory awareness or joy, just to give you some idea that you are still alive . . . But the sad fact is that this jazzing up more often becomes dangerous substitute activity, another phony therapy that prevents growth. (Perls, 1969, p. 1)

Functional methods of working with dreams are much more direct than Gestalt methods. We focus on the way the dreamer is in the dream and how he or she can change. Perls was working toward this emphasis when he suggested that people act out the different images and characters of their dreams. The problem with his method is that it remains embedded in dream content, just as free association and amplification methods focus too much on dream content. It is much more effective and efficient to focus directly on the emotional traits of a dreamer in a dream rather than on the contents of a dream.[3]

Perls' form of psychotherapy is usually identified as a "here and now" psychology. He placed all his emphasis on feeling and showing what is happening at the moment. He cared little about the person's past or plans for the future. We can understand and sympathize with this emphasis, for the past or the future of most people is unclear because they do not have a clear present.

It is possible to have real feelings about one's past, and even to partially relive times out of one's past. It is also possible to have real feelings about one's future based, not upon images, but upon the feeling choices in the present. We therefore distinguish between a person's sense of his *lifetime,* how he feels right here and now, and his sense of his *life span* (past, present and future). The two feeling awarenesses are related. Without a clear and vital sense of one's life as it is, one does

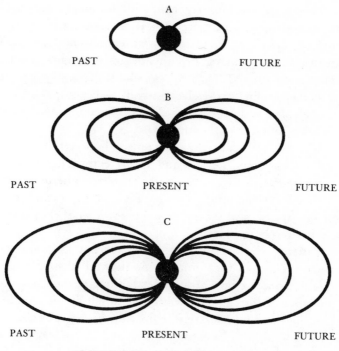

A

PAST   FUTURE

B

PAST   PRESENT   FUTURE

C

PAST   PRESENT   FUTURE

LIFETIMES AND LIFE SPANS

not have much true sense of how life was or how life in the future is dependent on how one lives now. We can represent the relationship between lifetime and life span schematically in the illustration on the following page.

Person "A" has a small sense of his life now, and a correspondingly small sense of his life as it was and will be in the future. He is often repressed because he is still unconscious of the way his past has taken present choices away from him. He is often forgetful because he has so little opportunity to consciously choose more expression in the present. Most of the time he lives from mixed-up images, images that were true to his past but false for his present. His future is limited to recurrences and not defined by his wants and feelings.

Person "B" sustains her feeling life for longer periods and consequently can span more of her past and her future. She would be capable of transformative dreaming because she has transformed her waking life and begun to unmix her past, present and future. Person "C" is capable of very long periods of sustained feeling expressiveness and has encompassed much of his past. His actions are now closely related to what he wants for his development in the future.

We can illustrate the differences between these three hypothetical people (A, B, and C) by comparing how they would respond to two simple tasks that we sometimes use in Functional Psychotherapy groups. First we ask people to tell their life stories, and second to write down what they want in five years and in ten years.

Patients who are just beginning therapy go about both of these tasks from their images. As they tell their life stories it is easy to observe how little understanding of their pasts they actually have. Instead they will begin to tell about something in their past and immediately be the way they were as children. They are unable to disentangle *now* and *then,* because they cannot sustain themselves in the present. They become similarly confused when they talk about five- and ten-year goals. They shift into "shoulds" and "maybes" instead of expressing their wants. They are incapable of picturing their future.

In contrast, very experienced patients (who have been in therapy three or four years) are able to talk evocatively about their pasts without reverting to past images. In a parallel way, they are able to make plans and set goals for their futures based upon what they feel and want for themselves.

"C" people have all types of dreams: dreams about their past, dreams about their present, dreams about their future, transformational dreams, symbolic dreams, power dreams, big dreams, and little dreams. They are capable of a range of dreaming which corresponds to their waking capabilities. New patients have dreams which are typically mixed up, just as their life stories and life plans are mixed up. Their dreams are usually symbolic, passive and vaguely anxious—in short the typical "normal dream."

In Freudian psychology, patients lose significant portions of their lifetimes through a preoccupation with symbols and past meanings. The danger of Jungian psychology is that symbols become expanded to contain feelings because active imagination by itself does not lead to the contact necessary to sustain feeling. The expansion into the future is not matched by a personal and real movement into the patient's past. In Gestalt Therapy,[4] an overfocus on acting the dream parts leads to unrelated actions. Without a unifying vision, Gestalt patients lose their life spans. A theorist who tried to avoid these dangers by "knowing the dream as it is" was Medard Boss.

THE DREAM ITSELF:
THE EXISTENTIAL THEORIES
OF MEDARD BOSS

The historian Wyss (1966) distinguishes between Freud's "reductive" methods, Jung's "amplification" methods and the "phenomenological" methods of existential analysis. These phenomenological methods were most clearly applied to dreams by Medard Boss.

Boss, like Jung and Freud, immersed himself in dreams. He reports, "During twenty-five years of practice as a psychotherapist I have been told about 50,000 dreams by at least 500 different people" (Boss, *The Analysis of Dreams,* 1958, p. 9). His basic criticism of most other clinicians and dream theory is that "all of them agreed with Freud's original dream theory in that they replaced the immediate and direct phenomenon by explanations of it. They saw in dreams the expression of something else, something merely assumed to exist behind the phenomena, some mental construct" (Boss, 1958, p. 9).

By stressing the continuity of dreaming and waking and by emphasizing that dreams are always *in relationship* to waking events and do not have a night-to-night historical continuity of their own, Boss comes very close to stating our parallelism hypothesis and the completion principle.

> . . . stereotype dreams will always return in like form, so long as life historical problems they contain are not adequately experienced as such in the dreamer's waking life, there to be faced, resolved and matured or at least developed. True, a dream event may have a certain history of its own, since all dreaming too is a form of existing . . . man, as a mere dreamer, cannot have a continuous development of his life. There is no dreamt life history running parallel to his waking life history. (Boss, 1958, p. 210)

Dream life parallels waking life, dreams try to resolve inadequately experienced waking events. Boss deepens this by emphasizing the waking structure of existence.

> A waking life is accordingly presupposed in all dream interpretation. Consequently, all possibilities of determining the essence of the dream in the dimension of waking life must be changed according to our insights into the peculiarities of the waking state, and all our understanding of the dream must fully depend on our particular understanding of waking existence . . . dreams themselves force all future investigations to pay heed to the structure of waking life, instead of taking it for granted. (Boss, 1958, pp. 210–11)

Boss says that "man, as a mere dreamer, cannot have a continuous development of his life." He does not see that neither can man as a mere *waking dreamer* have a continuous development of his life. Most people most of the time are not continuing their lives when they are awake. Instead they are re-dreaming their lives. They do not express how they feel, they symbolize how they feel and then repeat some automatic reactions over and over. Their lives go on but do not develop. They have little lifetime and a narrow life span. What they have instead is a life-style, acquired from fashions, and external images, and not based on inner feelings.

The limitations of Boss' "dream-in-itself" approach are inherent more in the structure of existential psychotherapy than in his theory. Simply telling a dream to another person can be a very powerful way of bringing dreams into waking life if that other person is a significant participant in the dreamer's waking life. This requires an experience beyond the solo practitioner structure of existential psychotherapy.

ROLLO MAY AND ERNEST ROSSI

Rollo May and Ernest Rossi are modern-day exponents of the existentialist-phenomenological approach to dreaming.[5] Both of them make some significant extensions and additions to Boss' theories. Their special significance for our functional approach is the emphasis they make on the unconscious as a *potentiality* and not just a memory: "I define unconsciousness here as the potentialities for awareness and experience which the individual is unable or unwilling at that time to actualize" (Caligor and May, *Dreams and Symbols*, 1968, p. 6). In doing this, they provide a vision, and a state of deepened awareness.

The similarity between May and Boss is evident in the following:

> What I am arguing is that unconscious life is also *intentional*. It is oriented in some direction . . . That is quite different from what has generally been assumed in psychoanalysis, that by *interpreting* the dream we give it meaning; for interpreting has tended

to be our transforming the dream into our symbols, rather than listening for the dream's symbols; interpreting it in our formulations, rationalizing it in terms of our particular school. Then lo and behold the meaning of the dream turns out at worst to be the therapist's meaning rather than the patient's, or at best the patient's formulation in terms and categories he has learned from the therapist. What I am proposing is something different: namely that the unconscious experience itself is intentional, moves toward meaning. It is *protentive* to borrow Hussert's term. (Caligor and May, 1968, p. 8)

We accept the existential emphasis on the dream itself by having patients simply tell one another their dreams without necessarily trying to say what they are about. By doing this they include each other in their waking life and dream life. But we differ from the existential position in two ways. We emphasize expression to keep the dream alive, to allow the feeling in the dream to extend into waking. Second, we recognize that dreams can tell us about the functional limits of a person's feeling life, where and how expression stopped and where it needs to get started.

One of the authors of this book has reported to us how he had been struggling to write sections of this chapter when it was in the third draft stage.

I felt very lethargic all day. Thinking and writing seemed impossibly difficult. I started to be really hard on myself and that made me feel even worse. Finally I went to talk with Riggs and he helped me to express all the feelings and crazy thoughts I was having: "I can't think. I feel dull. I should be able to do this. I won't be able to do this. I won't be able to finish. There's something wrong with me. I feel tired, just very tired." He didn't give me any advice but I decided to just give in to the tiredness and go to sleep. I awoke two hours later feeling refreshed and clear. Even more, I awoke out of a dream in which I was writing a section about Boss and I knew very clearly in the dream how to bring out the differences and similarities between the existential approach and our approach. I wrote three pages of notes down from my dream thoughts and went on to write that section the next day.

What is evident in this report is how the dreamer, by relating to the people around him and showing how he was feeling, was able to relate to his own feelings in a positive instead of a punishing way. He then went on to develop in his dream the ideas which are discussed in this chapter. Waking and dreaming became interrelated for him, just as they are for anyone, through expression.

By focusing on the dream itself, the existentialists lose the life of a dream as surely as the analysts who search for meanings behind the dream. A dream is, in itself, dead; only when it is expressed to another person does it acquire living consequences.

It is not the dream in itself that is of greatest importance, but *how the dreamer relates to how he is in the dream.* If he perceives the way he is functioning and becomes aware of the similarities to daily life, and if he shares the experience with people by telling it, then he relates the dream to himself and to others. The first concern is not whether the dream pictures are subjectively understood, objectively understood, or transformed, but rather that they are shared, whether derived from dreams, thoughts, fantasies, or waking events.

The three theorists we discussed in this chapter all contributed toward a transformative way of working with and thinking about dreams. Jung stressed the prospective function of dream symbols and showed how dream images can develop within a dream series. Perls emphasized affective expression as the crucial entry point into feeling and living what dreams mean. Boss returned again and again to the simple, yet easily overlooked message, that the dream is complete in itself—the dream is the dream is the dream. Boss makes clear that the dream needs no interpretation beyond itself, it needs only to be brought into relationship with the dreamer's waking life.

So what is missing? Why did Jung and Perls and Boss not arrive at a complete functional and transformative approach to dreams? We suggest that the missing component is not some understanding of dreams but more sharing and living of dreams. Long-term transformations in dreams for individuals cannot be achieved or sustained without the support of a community. Individual therapy sessions and workshops are inadequate to bring about the major transformations which are possible. Perhaps if Jung and Perls and Boss and their colleagues and patients had all lived together and shared their dreams, they would have discovered how to go beyond solo dreaming. Perls anticipated this limitation.

> Two years ago I read a paper at the American Psychological Association. I claimed all individual therapy to be obsolete, and pointed out the advantages of the workshop. I believe that in the workshop, you learn so much by understanding what's going on in this other person, and realize so much of his conflicts are your own, and by identification you learn . . . Now I'm slowly coming to the insight that workshops and group therapy also are obsolete, and we are going to start our first Gestalt kibbutz next year . . . We hope we can . . . produce *real* people, people who are willing to take a stand, people who are willing to take responsibility for their lives. (Perls, 1969, *Gestalt Therapy Verbatim*, pp. 73-74)

Unfortunately Perls died before he could live out the

possibilities of his Gestalt community. To learn more about the influence of communities on dream transformation we will need to look beyond the boundaries of our culture at communities where dreams are not just discussed but lived.

6

TWO DREAMER COMMUNITIES: THE AMERICAN IROQUOIS AND THE SENOI OF MALAYSIA

Sound of the bell, sound of the heart
My brothers
My sisters
I am meeting you
I am meeting you at the dance
(Washat Song from Relander,
Drummers and Dreamers, 1957, p. 84)

It would be a mistake to read about the Iroquois and the Senoi and conclude that it is necessary to seek visions, compose dream songs, and participate in dream dances in order to work with dreams functionally. These techniques are of no more or less value than the techniques of associating, amplifying, or extending a dream dialogue. The important conclusion, which we will state before we have even offered all the arguments, is that it is the attitude of making the private public which is the most important feature of dreamer communities. There are other features of importance which we will also discuss, but this attitude is primary.

To the transplanted European mind it seemed perfectly plausible that when American Indian tribes were located in reservations, they should be split into groups different from the tribal groups they had known all their lives. To the Indians it seemed like madness, a decision of the head, not of the heart. It saddened and then destroyed them, because it destroyed the basis for their community.

> "On our reservation no man dares to sing . . . soon all the songs will be forgotten. White people do not like us to sing Indian songs. They think our songs are bad . . ."
>
> "And how did you make your songs?" the Chief was asked.
>
> "We dreamed them," was the answer. "When a man would go away by himself—off into the solitude—then he would dream a song."
>
> "And do men still dream songs?"
>
> "If they do, they do not tell. White people do not like it. But if a man has dreamed a song, he may take another man quietly aside and teach the song to him. His song will not be so soon forgotten if one other has it as well as himself."
>
> (Curtis, 1950, *The Indian's Book,* p. 314)

This Pomo chief is expressing an attitude toward dreaming and dreams. It is an attitude which directs us to include other people in our lives by telling them our dreams and by participating in songs and dances and projects that emerge from dreams. It is a crucial part of belonging to a community. What is most important about this attitude is that it emphasizes the sharing of *internal* events. That most private of experiences—a dream—is made public.[1] This is the way we need to go to discover a new kind of dream and dreamer beyond the theories.

THE IROQUOIS

There are many interesting American Indian dream communities, but we will focus on the Iroquois because they developed dream methods and theories which clearly paralleled those of modern psychotherapy.[2] Most of our information about the Iroquois is drawn from the writings of the anthropologist Anthony Wallace, who based his studies on the journals of 17th century Jesuit missionaries.

Wallace comments on the remarkable similarity of Freudian and Iroquoian theories.

> While it is evident that the Iroquoian and Freudian dream theory are not precisely the same (the Iroquoian theory introduced an animistic thesis as well as the psychoanalytic one), the differences are not much more marked than the differences between, for instance, Jungian and Freudian varieties of psychoanalytic theory (Wallace, 1967, p. 172) . . . Psychoanalytic in this usage thus includes only the theory of dreams which regards the dream as the symbolic expression of the unconscious wishes. (Wallace in Middleton, *Magic, Witchcraft, and Curing*, 1967, p. 171)

Considering the many differences between 17th century Iroquois society and 19th century Vienna, the similarity in dream theories is remarkable. A description of Iroquoian theory is given by the Jesuit Father Ragueneau in 1649:

> In addition to the desires which we generally have that are free, or at least voluntary in us, (they) . . . believe that our souls have other desires, which are, as it were, inborn and concealed. These, they say, come from the depths of the soul, not through any knowledge, but by means of a certain blind trans-

porting of the soul to certain objects . . . Now they believe that our soul makes these natural desires known by means of dreams, which are its language. Accordingly when these desires are accomplished, it is satisfied; but, on the contrary, if it not be granted what it desires, it becomes angry, and not only does not give its body the good and the happiness that it wished to procure for it, but often it also revolts against the body, causing various diseases, and even death. (From Wallace, 1967, pp. 174-5)

Wallace describes the sophisticated way in which the Iroquois discriminated between the latent and manifest content of dreams:

They recognized conscious and unconscious parts of the mind. They knew the great force of unconscious desires and were aware that the frustration of these desires could cause mental and physical ("psychosomatic") illness. They understood that these desires were expressed in symbolic form by dreams, but that the individual could not always properly interpret these dreams himself. They had noted the distinction between the manifest and latent content of dreams, and employed what sounds like the technique of free association to uncover the latent meaning. And they considered that the best method for the relief of psychic and psychosomatic distress was to give the frustrated desire satisfaction, either directly or symbolically. (Wallace, 1967, pp. 176-7)

People who are acquainted with Freud's work only from his theoretical writings might object to aligning the practical bent that the Iroquois took with dreams with the psychoanalytic emphasis on insight and sublimation. But it is clear from Freud's case writings (see especially *The Wolf Man*, 1971) that he took a very practical approach with his patients. He didn't indulge in interpreting the meaning of bread in dreams when his patients were hungry and poor. Freud often took a direct therapeutic approach and loaned patients money, helped them to get jobs and gave them practical advice.

PERSONAL AND TRANSPERSONAL DREAMS

In some ways the Iroquois combined both the Freudian and the Jungian approaches to dreams. They distinguished between symptomatic or personal dreams and visitation or transpersonal dreams.

> A symptomatic dream expressed a wish of the dreamer's soul. This wish was interpreted either by the dreamer himself or by a clairvoyant (Wallace, 1967, p. 185) . . . These diagnoses served as signals for the execution of various rather conventional patterns of acting out the wish, either literally or symbolically (Wallace, 1967, p. 186) . . . The second category of dreams showed powerful supernatural beings who usually spoke personally to the dreamer, giving him a message of importance for himself and often also for the whole community. Sometimes these were personality transformation dreams, in which the language, doubts, and conflicts of the dreamer emerged from his vision with a new sense of dignity, a new capacity for playing a hitherto difficult role, and a new feeling of health and well-being. (Wallace, 1967, p. 187)

These visitation dreams are clearly very similar to the ancient Aesclepian healing dreams of the Greeks (see Meier, 1967). We interpret them within the transformative orientation as big dreams which signal a need for the dreamer, and often his immediate community, to shift their level of feeling in order to cope with major problems and situations within the dreamer's life.

The Iroquois recognized the importance of this dream signal, and the total community often became involved in visitation dreams.

> . . . dreams in which such powerful personages as Torachiawazon (culture hero and favorite dream figure) appeared and announced they wanted something done (frequently for the dreamer) were matters of national moment. Clairvoyants were called upon; the chiefs met and discussed ways of satisfying the sometimes expensive or awkward demands of the dreamers (representing the power above), or of averting the predicted catastrophe. Not infrequently this type of dream also bore elements of personality transformation for the dreamer, who in his identification with the gods assumed a new role as prophet, messiah, public censor and advisor. Such prophets might make detailed recommendations about the storage of crops, the waging of war, diplomatic policy toward other tribes and toward the French or the English, measures to avert epidemics or famine. Rarely, however, did such projects maintain a lasting influence. (Wallace, 1967, pp. 188-9)

The importance of visitation and myth-making has not dissipated, but contemporary society is too diversified for dreamers to be visited by one dream figure such as Torachiawazon, the favorite dream figure of the Iroquois. The figures who appear in big dreams today are much more like the archetypal figures described by Jung. However, within our own small dreamer community, we have noticed that some of the therapists begin to appear as visitation figures in each other's dreams and in the dreams of their patients. In some ways it is an advantage to have divine images in common, because

everyone in the society will recognize a dream's importance—
for the dreamer and the community. In other ways it is more
desirable to have visitations from dream figures who can actually be consulted in waking.

To understand the Iroquois, it is important to understand
the role of myth-making in any society. In a highly diversified
and individualistic society, every dreamer becomes his own
myth-maker. The disadvantages of this individualism is that
there are no shared cultural heroes with enough numinosity
to signify everyone in society's need for transformation. Within
our own dream community real life figures of importance to
the community member (such as therapists or close friends)
take on mythic importance in some dreams. This is a potentially dangerous social phenomenon if the power of the dream
figures continues to be projected outward onto them once the
dreamer has awakened. Dreamers must be helped to absorb
their own symbols so that they perceive that it is they who have
made the therapists into symbols for their own power and
feelings.

If the symbol is reabsorbed, the power and feeling behind
the mythic visitor becomes democratized, or incorporated into
the dreamer and subsequently shared with the community.
Without democratization, this feeling and power is invested
or projected on the person, or even into the dreamer's social
environment. Unavailable to the dreamer, it becomes lost to
the community. In the following paragraph, Campbell calls
this democratization process "creative mythology."

> In the context of a traditional mythology the symbols
> are presented in socially maintained rites, through
> which the individual is required to experience, or will
> pretend to have experienced, certain insights, senti-
> ments, and commitments. In what I am calling
> "creative" mythology, on the other hand, this order
> is reversed; the individual has had an experience of

his own—of order, horror, beauty, or even mere exhilaration—which he seeks to communicate through signs; and if his realization has been of a certain depth and import, his communication will have the value and force of living myth—for those, that is to say, who receive and respond to it of themselves, with recognition, uncoerced. (Campbell, 1968, p. 4)

The kind of democratization of myth-making Campbell talks about requires both individualism and community. We believe that the Iroquois were too limited by their attachments to traditional mythic heroes to progress psychologically all the way to creative myth-making. As we have described previously, the semi-tribes of Freudians and Jungians, in contrast, were too limited by individualism, with too little interpersonal sharing to be able to sustain mythically important dreams. The Iroquois had their own psychotherapists, specialists in helping tribal members understand and act from their dreams. Father Jouvency wrote about them in 1610:

For the purpose of ascertaining desires and innate appetites of this character, they summon soothsayers, who, as they think, have a divinely-imparted power to look into the inmost recesses of the mind. These men declare that whatever first occurs to them, or something from which they suspect some gain can be derived, is desired by the sick person. Thereupon the parents, friends, and relatives of the patient do not hesitate to procure and lavish upon him whatever it may be, however expensive, a return of which is never thereafter to be sought . . . (Wallace in *Magic, Witchcraft and Curing*, 1967, p. 176)

Notice that the Iroquois psychotherapist involved the relatives of the patient in helping to work out the dreamer's needs and wishes. They did then what is now called Family Therapy and Community Psychology.

The Jesuits had difficulty comprehending the Iroquois dream theory and techniques, specifically when the techniques sometimes led to the gratification of sexually aggressive desires.

> During the "Feast of Fools," the annual "Ononharia" or "turning the brain upside down," when men and women ran madly from cabin to cabin acting out their dreams in charades and demanding the dream be guessed or satisfied, many women and men alike dreamt of fighting natural enemies. Dreams in which hostility was directed at members of other nations were properly satisfied by acting them out both in pantomime and in real life; but bad dreams about members of the same community were acted out only in some symbolic form, which had a prophylactic effect. (Wallace, 1967, p. 180)

Our own view of the Iroquois' methods is much more sanguine than that of the Jesuits. Indeed, we believe the Jesuits might well have benefited by having their brains "turned upside down." We have found that dreams often provide an entry into a kind of "conscious craziness" which allows patients to experience their defenses and images. This often helps them live in new ways beyond images and from feelings.

THE RIDDLE TECHNIQUE

The riddle technique was a method for working with dreams. It was described by Father LeJeune in 1639:

> During the dream guessing rites at Midwinter and, on occasion of illness at other times of the year, persons propounded Riddles in a sacred game. Each person or a group announced his "own and special desire or 'Ondinonc' — according as he is able to get information and enlightenment by dreams — not openly, however, but through Riddles. For example,

someone will say, 'What I desire and what I am seeking is that which bears a lake within itself'; and by this is intended a pumpkin or calabash. Another will say, 'What I ask for is seen in my eyes—it will be marked with various colors'; and because the same Huron word that signifies 'eye' also signified 'glass bead', this is a clue to divine what he desires—namely, some kind of beads of this material and of different colors. Another will intimate that he desires an Andacwandat feast—that is to say, many fornications and adulteries. His Riddle being guessed, there is no lack of persons to satisfy his desire." (Wallace, 1967, p. 178)

The psychological acumen displayed by this riddle technique can be appreciated if we think about the psychoanalytic emphasis on the connections between jokes and unconscious wishes. It takes a sophisticated intelligence to play the riddle game with dreams. This is one example of how Iroquois dream techniques actually surpassed later psychoanalytic techniques. The riddle techniques emerged from a culture that was in some ways more expressive than Freud's Vienna or Jung's Zurich.

THE PRIMACY OF THE DREAM

The importance of dreams to the Iroquois community would be hard to overestimate. Father Fremin wrote in 1668:

The Iroquois have, properly speaking, only a single Divinity—the dream. To it they render their submission, and follow all its orders with the utmost exactness. The Tsonnotouens (Seneca) are more attached to this superstition than any of the others; their Religion in this respect becomes even a matter of scruple; whatever it be that they think they have done in their dreams, they believe themselves (absolutely

obliged) to execute at the earliest moment . . . They (the Seneca) spare no pains, no industry, to show their attachment thereto, and their folly in this particular goes to such an excess as would be hard to imagine. He who has dreamed during the night that he was bathing, runs immediately, as soon as he rises, all naked, to several cabins, in each of which he has a kettleful of water thrown over his body, however cold the weather may be. Another who has dreamed that he was taken prisoner and burned alive, has found himself bound and burned like a captive on the next day, being persuaded that by thus satisfying his dream, this fidelity will avert from him the pain and infamy of his captivity and death, — which, according to what he has learned from his Divinity, he is otherwise bound to suffer among his enemies. Some have been known to go as far as Quebec, travelling a hundred and fifty leagues, for the sake of getting a dog that they had dreamed of buying there . . .
(Wallace, 1967, p. 173)

It would be easy to dismiss the dreamer's or the community's response to the dream as excessive. But these extreme cases were meant to show only how extensively the dreamer and the community were involved with the dream. We could state that the Iroquois were misled in that they literally followed the dream. Again, there is a similarity to Freudian theory and practice, where a dream is pursued to a literal message. Neither understood that a dream is a picture of a feeling of most importance for what it shows about the way the dreamer is functioning emotionally. However, this literal pursuit is not as important as the process of community that ensues.

Dreams are not to brood over, to analyze, or to prompt lonely and independent action; they are to be told, or at least hinted at, and it is for other people to be active. The community rallies round the dreamer with gifts and ritual. (Wallace, 1967, pp. 189–90)

The Iroquois community is as important for the dreamer as the dreams are for the community. In our estimation, the Iroquoian dream theory and techniques blended some of the best features of Freudian and Jungian analysis. And the Iroquian dream community was, in some ways, more refined than those developed by either Freud or Jung. There was more contact and expression within the community. Private was made public through sophisticated games, songs, dances, and the sharing of dreams. In fact, the doctor-patient relationship basically served to involve the community in the sharing process. The actual relationship between the dreamer and his Iroquian psychiatrist was clearly secondary.

From what we can gather from the writings of the Jesuits, the Iroquoian community, like the Freudian, never successfully made the full transition from the interpretation of dreams to the transformation of dreams. Transformation is totally dependent upon community structure and attitude which say, "What is most privately mine — my thoughts, wishes, fantasies and dreams — can be fully shared with everyone I know." There was an incomplete conversion of private life to public in the Iroquoian community.

They were limited by their literal devotion to acting out the content of their dreams. Like Freudian theory so much later, their dream religion remained essentially compensatory. The feeling contained in the pictures of their dreams was never fully shared. They shared the picture, but not the essential process that would change their dream and community life from compensatory to transformative.

Further, as dissimilar as Iroquoian and Viennese society were, they both were characterized by an emphasis on individual, independent achievement that limited the extent to which a full conversion of private to public could be made. Their society was intrinsically competitive, not cooperative. This limited the sharing and inclusion that must be an essential part of waking to be an essential part of dreaming. Wallace's description of the male ideal in Iroquois society would not be far off as a description of the European ideal.

> In their daily affairs, Iroquois men were brave, active, self-reliant and autonomous, they cringed to no one and begged for nothing. But no man can balance forever on such a pinnacle of masculinity, where asking and being given are unknown. . . . The culture of dreams may be regarded as a useful escape valve. . . . Iroquois men dreamt; and, without shame, they received the fruits of their dreams and their souls were satisfied. (Wallace, 1967, p. 190)

Compensatory dreams are the inevitable norm in a society where there is an incomplete conversion of private to public life. By being literal and sharing only the dream pictures, the Iroquois conversion was incomplete. This was reflected in the competitive, individualistic nature of the community. And this feature of the community prevented the sharing of feelings that were hidden in their dreams and rituals. They never achieved the sophistication of the Malaysian dreamer community which we will describe next.

THE SENOI OF MALAYSIA[3]

At the same time that Freud and Jung were beginning to solidly establish their reputations as the leading dream experts and theoreticians in the Western Hemisphere, the most sophisticated dream psychologists in the world had just been discovered in the primitive jungles of Malaysia by two young men.

Kilton Stewart, an American anthropologist and psychologist, and H. D. Noone, an ethnographer sent by the British government, were amazed to find a group of Malay aboriginals who had succeeded in creating a culture of peace and harmony based upon working with dreams. Stewart and Noone studied and lived with the Senoi dream people during 1934 and 1937. They found the Senoi to be a strikingly peaceful group who nevertheless dominated the other primitive people around them. Indeed, the Senoi impressed Stewart and Noone in the same way that they did their jungle neighbors, by the power and intensity of their dreams.

To understand the power of the Senoi dream, you must fully understand the power and radical nature of their community. The beginning of this understanding can come from a simple observation of how their community was structured.

COMMUNITY STRUCTURE

The typical Senoi settlement usually contained 50 to 200 people and was strung out along high ground near a river. Most of these communities had one "long house" which provided a place for ceremonial activities. The long house was often supplemented by smaller dwelling units, each of which contained a small extended or nuclear family.

The physical layout of these settlements accurately describes a cornerstone of Senoi society. The large long house was the primary area of the community, the area of sharing. It was in close proximity to the smaller living areas. There was no seat of government, no distant authority nor a structure to house it.

> The house is like a whole village under one roof; in the centre is the dancing floor of split bamboo, framed along four sides by twenty separate family compartments, each screened off and opening onto a fire hearth of beaten earth. (Noone, *Temiar Dream Songs from Malaya,* 1955, Album and Album Notes, p. 3)

Every structure enhanced the strong sense of belonging to the community. Both time and space were carefully reserved for sharing. This mundane fact can be passed over as some form of primitivism, yet it was the basis of a powerful, sophisticated system of psychology that worked. Who would argue with the fact of the failure of our own private society to provide such a system? Since we have little time and few places for communing in our society, we go outside our community for this sharing, usually to an office of a strange shaman. This results in a concept of psychology where the system always seems outside of the way we normally live. We subject ourselves to a psychoanalytic system, a gestalt system, a bioenergetic system, but it is external, not part of our life at home.

The lack of internal sharing within the community leads to the use of outside authority in our modern or technological society. We have external systems for advice, healing, protection, and government. It is interesting to contrast this description with the following one entitled "Socio-Political Organization" from a Malaysian government publication.

> Division of labor is normally flexible and each family sets its own norms. Each community has its own "saka" or "communal area" and a Senoi will always have a deep sense of belonging to his "saka." (Idris, "A Brief Note on the Orang Asli of West Malaysia and Their Administration," 1972, p. 4)

This sense of belonging and being totally part of the community led to rule not through laws and external enforcement agencies, but rule through direct contact. The sanctions were verbal and expressive rather than written and restrictive. Traditionally, the Senoi were ruled by a group of elders and the society had strict taboos on violence.

Although they were ruled by a group of elders, our emphasis should be on the fact of group leadership. Their emphasis on community virtually eliminated "headmen, or chiefs, or any form of fixed authority" (Stewart, "Magico-religious beliefs and practices in primitive society," Ph.D. dissertation, London School of Economics, 1947, p. 177). Although authority exists, it too was shared. Everyone exercised his own authority.

> One impressive feature of the authority structure of Temiar shamans is the manner in which the leadership of the ceremonial spirts shifts from hour to hour to different individuals, young and old alike, and the way in which all members of the group agree and cooperate with the momentary leader. (Stewart, 1947, p. 177)

The shifting of leadership precluded any ascendancy of leadership in spiritual matters. Unlike the Iroquois and the Freudian tribes with their shaman or psychiatrist, the Senoi shared leadership.

Stewart stated clearly that since there was no hereditary authority in the Senoi priesthood, each individual accepted as final authority the person who was personally appealing and encountered most often as a dream visitation figure. Whoever had the greatest authority when controversial matters arose was counted as the leading shaman of the long house. This sharing strengthened each individual as well as the community. Everyone in the society contributed, enriching the community which in turn gave to each individual. In this manner, sharing both produced and at the same time evolved from a psychology that was distinctly unique and effective.

TRANSLATIONS

To fully appreciate the Senoi community, and before we discuss their psychology, we must make a number of translations. Anthropological translations of some Senoi terms produced misleading impressions. For example, a Western reader is not likely to pay much respectful attention to a culture that has "taboos" and concerns itself with dream "spirits" and dream "trances." However, the word "taboo" immediately takes on another meaning if we translate it as "feeling guideline."

Taboos. In the Senoi culture, it was taboo to think or dream or do harmful things to one's fellows. This "feeling guideline" suggested that each individual was solely responsible for his thoughts and dreams. If a man used goodwill in meeting with his friends during the day, this was reflected in his dreams at night. This "guideline" leads to the following:

> The Senoi believe that any human being, with the aid of his fellows, can outface, master, and actually utilize all beings and forces in the dream universe. His experience leads him to believe that, if you cooperate with your fellows or oppose them with goodwill in the daytime, their images will help you in your dreams, and that every person should be the supreme ruler and master of his own dream or spiritual universe and can demand and receive the help and cooperation of all the forces there. (Stewart in Tart, *Altered States of Consciousness*, 1969, p. 62)

This individual, as sole ruler and master, had a guideline which helped him to demand and receive help and cooperation by requiring him to openly expose his thoughts with goodwill so that there could be social interaction.

This is in contrast to the taboos of Western Civilization in which we taboo actions, but not thoughts or dreams. The thoughts and dreams remain secrets, beyond the province of community interest, and the individual feels no outward responsibility for them. This taboo preserves the distinction of public and private, while the Senoi taboo, described above, broke down this distinction. They designed feeling guidelines which are in accord with our parallelism principle. Only when waking is filled with the power of exposure and goodwill, can dreaming reflect that power and mastery. When waking imitates dreaming and dreaming imitates waking, full dream mastery occurs.

Spirits. In Senoi dream psychology, spirits were simply symbols for feelings, feelings similar to those we experienced as children lying in the dark, and staring out at the shadows that surrounded us. We think that the Senoi's translation of "feeling" to "spirit" was functional. It gave the Senoi a common way of talking about feelings, much in the same way anyone in any type of psychotherapy learns to describe what is happening to him or her.

> Although children can stay up as late as they like most of them are asleep by about eight o'clock. Visitors have usually gone home by this time, since people are rather uneasy about being outdoors after dark. Their unease is justified. After nightfall, wild animals like the tiger . . . sometimes enter a settlement. Besides wild animals, the Senoi say "gangsters," "evil spirits" and "death spirits" are abroad at night. (Dentan, *The Semai: A Nonviolent People of Malaysia*, 1968, p. 54)

The word "spirit" can even be further translated as "feeling complex" or "feeling projection." Spirits appear in dreams in two ways. First, when feelings have been left incomplete during the day, they get disguised as a spirit or "feeling complex." Secondly, a spirit can occur as a "feeling projection" in the case of the prospective dream, when a new level of feeling integration is required. The feeling is symbolized because it is not yet physically attained, felt, and expressed by the dreamer.

Trances. When a Senoi man had an important prospective dream, he shared it with other people in the group first by telling them about it, and then by leading the group members through a dream dance. During this dance, the participants began to feel what the dreamer experienced in his dream. This could be dismissed as a "trance," but we prefer to call it a "guided reverie." By making a "guided reverie," the dreamer is making available his expanded range of feeling and power to the whole community.

COMMUNITY SUPPORT

It is not the dream that made Senoi psychology unique, but the community that supported that dream. Perhaps the greatest psychological technique developed by the Senoi was the daily time set aside for communing. The time of communing took away any specialness about dreams. It reduced dreams to nighttime acts which could be talked about and changed, nighttime acts which had a past, present, and future significance for daytime life.

> Everyone's dream is acceptable and should be expressed since each dreamer may be a vessel of supernatural aid or warnings. During the interpretation and discussion of these dreams which determine the saka's agenda and activity, the children and younger men become familiar with the words and concepts applied to the various dreams, with the philosophy behind interpretation, and are furnished a stimulus toward remembering their own dreams . . . As will be seen, the Temiar do not look at the dream as an experience by itself. It is the result and resolution of something which has happened before, the end of something; or it is the beginning of something which should be continued in waking life. Or it is a warning against or guide for something planned or already in the process of execution. (Stewart, 1947, p. 104)

Stewart saw both the dream and the necessity of communing. This becomes apparent when he discusses what he calls the twofold nature of Senoi psychology. "Senoi psychology falls into two categories. The first deals with dream interpretation; the second with the dream expression in the agreement trance or cooperative reverie" (Stewart in Tart, 1969, p. 161). It is not interpretation that makes the psychology work. What is important is that time is taken out solely for the purpose of expressing the dream. As Stewart noted, without direction and expression the dream itself was not enough to form the society. "As long as it is undirected, dreaming is a releasing, balancing process which works less and less efficiently as the personality becomes more complicated with increasing age" (Stewart, "The Dream Comes of Age," *Mental Hygiene*, 1962, p. 234).

What was necessary was a form of "living interpretation." Making public private thoughts leads to making public every thought. Senoi dream interpretation was a way of life. It would be difficult to imagine a psychoanalyst getting up from his chair and following his patient in a dream dance. Psychoanalysis is not a way of life. The Senoi dream interpretation was, because the community did not just interpret, but interacted with the dreamer. Through instructions, dances and reveries, the communal response was not a second feature of a twofold psychology. It was an extension of the single nature of their psychology, the necessity of communing.

The Senoi were careful to educate their children to be full participants in the communing process. Like everything else, the educational process was integrated into the Senoi way of life within a community. Their children did not attend lectures or enter primitive schools in order to be initiated into the community.

In the same manner each twenty-four hour period was an integration of day and night, of dreaming and waking. In fact, Stewart described how the Senoi regarded the activities of the day and night as part of an inseparable unit in which one corrected mistakes of the day in one's dreams and the dream mistakes in daytime and in future dreams.

The Senoi understood the parallelism between waking and dreaming. When we began reading about the Senoi, before we studied them seriously, we were eager to have big dreams, life-changing dreams, and dreams which showed shamanistic qualities (Hart, "Dreams in the Classroom," in *Experiment and Innovation,* 1971, IV, p. 51–66). The illusion we had is similar to that of most people studying dreams. Dreams can be life-changing, but primarily, dreams are dreams. When a person begins to change his or her life it will be reflected in his or her dreams. This creates a dynamic between waking and dreaming which allows interaction between them. In the Senoi educational process dreams were talked about, but it was waking behavior that was changed.

The need for education can be clearly seen when we talk about the *power dream,* a type of dream that the Senoi cultivated. As we have already described, in power dreams the dreamer does things that he could not do in reality. He may breathe underwater, fly, die and be reborn, or do other supernatural feats. These extraordinary dreams are largely ignored by all but esoteric cults in our society, but among the Senoi they were prized, and the children were taught to dream for power.

Stewart described in detail how the child was held responsible for his actions in his dreams. If his friends were present, he was to be of service to them. If he saw new and interesting places, he was encouraged to remember what he saw and find out if there was anything of value there for the community. If he saw animals or monsters which blocked his way, he was taught to attack them and match his strength with theirs. Stewart points out that the Senoi criticism of dream behavior, whether positive or negative, implied that the child could change his behavior in the future. This allowed him to act differently in future dreams because of the criticism or encouragement he received. Stewart found that the child did act differently when he was awake because of the criticism, and it was a matter of common occurrence that he also acted differently in his dreams.

Power dreams are important because they can indicate that the dreamer is fully expressing his feelings. But power dreams, like prospective dreams, are indicators of psychological health only when they are accompanied by full expressiveness, complete activity, and strong feelings in waking. Without these features, they are of little importance.[4] The Senoi recognized this fact very clearly; their children were guided to be active and fully expressive in all dream encounters. This guiding took place during the day so that it could occur during dreamlife as well.

> Implicit in these dream interpretations is the idea that a living man with a body, plus the friendly spirits of the world, has ultimate power over the forces of evil if he has the courage to make use of that power and the cooperation of other human beings. His souls cannot help him and other people well unless they can get free of his body. Fear makes his souls withdraw deeper and deeper into the body; and the greater the tension the more they are paralyzed. Unless they are free to move about, they cannot cooperate with each other and be led and directed by the *ruai*. Implicit in the idea of moving out of the body with the head soul is the further idea of cooperation, coordination and integration. These dream discussions, which the child hears, cause him to start watching for his own dreams and recounting them to his father and older brothers at the morning meal. (Stewart, 1947, p. 112)

The children were guided to make use of the power of their feelings and their thoughts. Stewart was not suggesting that the children were learning to become intellectually oriented, or "free of the body." When he described souls becoming withdrawn deeper and deeper into the body, he was describing the process of making the private even more private. When he talked about the souls being free to move about, the Senoi children were being guided to make the private public. This resulted in a sharing of dreams at the morning meal, the first step for a young child in becoming part of the community.

Dreamer education began for the child when he or she presented dreams to the parents. The child's dream was taken as a vivid and nonsymbolic representation of the child's needs and problems.

> The child is impressed by the fact that the adults do listen to his dreams and take them seriously, that they do trace them back to shocks, accidents, and conflicts of the day before, and that they do often modify their behavior and ask others to do so, on the basis of the data the dream presents (Stewart, "Mental Hygiene and World Peace," in *Mental Hygiene,* 38, No. 3, 1954, p. 401).

In response to the child's presentation, the Senoi parents took two complementary steps. First, they examined the waking reality as revealed in the child's dream. For example, if a child dreamed that his mother left him outside so that she could go in and hold a younger child, he would have been expressing a need that the mother was not fulfilling. The father then would take the child to the mother and tell her of the child's dream. The mother would then pay particular attention to the child. If she had been neglecting him, she would say it had been unintentional, and that she would attempt to look after him with closer attention.

Secondly, both the mother and father would instruct the child to become active in the dream. He would be told to face the dream mother, and to demand in the dream what he wanted. In this instance, he would bang on the door and call for help to his father and other community members. As the child would become active in his dream, he would begin to express more and free himself from both his symbolic dream mother and the dream feelings associated with her. His successful dealing with his dream mother would relieve him of unfelt feelings toward his waking mother. The waking mother's real response to his needs would help to stop the further development of other unmet needs.

In this way, the waking response of the parents and the sleeping actions of the child would combine to disengage the waking and sleeping dream work mechanisms. Freed of the symbols, the child would grow into an adult who was aware and awake. His dreams would become active and vividly non-symbolic. The dreams would tell him, with the help of his community, how to change his waking life and how to act differently in future dreams.

BECOMING ONE OF US

In the Senoi language, the word "Senoi" means "one of us." Dreamer education progressed with the maturation of the dreamer. It began with the child learning to deal with his frustrations. What was unique and often misunderstood was that the child learned because the Senoi family and community took the time to teach him. He did not learn by an isolated initiation ceremony like those of the American Indian, but steadily within a group setting.

> It is as though the frustrations of social life are expressed in dreams as frustrations, and the child is encouraged or forced by social pressure to resolve them in his sleep with the help of authorities and

symbols from the social world, just as he is encouraged to solve his problems of the daytime with the help of his dream characters. (Stewart, 1947, pp. 120–21)

The learning was easy and natural. This supported the child's growth, and not the growth of the ritual. As the child matured, he became more and more involved with authorities. The Senoi simply commented on each other's lives and actions, often using the time of dream interpretation to do so. Although the dream authorities usually went on acting like social authorities, the destructive dream characters became constructive and cooperative as maturation proceeded.

The trance was also a communal affair. The people of the tribe tested the trance as a form of fun and relaxation. We believe that the Senoi did not take their rites and rituals with metaphysical seriousness. They participated in them because they were of immediate benefit. The trance dances were forms of expressive behavior which unified the community and supported the individual's creativity and growth.

The trances served the individual and the community by extending the sharing of the dream far beyond the family and the first social authorities. In this way the community began to be involved in the child's testing of the reality of his dream. Each experience was tested with the community, and without community testing there was only ritual and fantasy. This testing out of their dreams on a social level from adolescence on made them differentiate clearly, according to Stewart, between objective and subjective reality.

As maturation was completed, the new member of the community was fully able to take part in all aspects of the Senoi leadership. There was no position among the Senoi that anyone could not attain, nor any individual who could not be challenged. The Senoi were not dependent on a ruler, but on communal ruling. From their practices, they learned that since there was no one in the waking world above them, there also was no one better or stronger than they in their dreams. They were a very democratic people. But they did not elect. Since they were willing to follow their feelings, they shared in governing themselves. In fact, Stewart's research showed that one of the most impressive features of the authority structure of the Temiar shamans was the manner in which the leadership of the ceremonial spirits shifted from hour to hour to different individuals, young and old alike, and the way in which all members of the group agreed and cooperated with the leader of the moment.

In this way the Senoi child grew up with an ever deepening experience of being one of a group, "one of us." It was this total experience which allowed the child to progress toward transformative dreaming. The same must be true in a psychotherapeutic community. Unless and until the patients in the community feel they are "one of us" they will be unable to be fully expressive in dreaming or in waking. There is no special trick of dream technology that the Senoi applied which can be quickly adopted by individuals or groups in our society. It was everything they did and thought about dreams and waking that made a difference, and educated Senoi children to dream transformative dreams.

THE STORY OF *ALONG* — A DREAM

The following episode described by Stewart illustrates that it was everything the Senoi did that was important, and not the magic contained in the dream. This story took the mystery away from the Senoi, and showed them as a people. *Along* was growing in importance as a hunter, and he had a dream which he presented to his colleagues.

> *Along* on the Piah organized a hunting expedition. He dreamed last night that he found a dead deer in the gulch leading from a salt spring, a three-hour

walk from the long house. He was examining the
bile sac in the dream and discovered a slight irregu-
larity like a claw in the left-hand side near the tip.
Along felt the dream was a good omen and that the
party would find the deer in the gulch where his
dream had pictured it. (Stewart, 1947, p. 105)

Not everyone agreed with this interpretation and so some men
stayed and worked on the gardens.

At night, when the hunting party returned, they felt
the meaning of the dream was more clear. They had
bagged two flying foxes and a porcupine. The hunting was successful, but not outstandingly so. . . .
Since tracks could always be found in that particular
gulch, the dream seemed important to Noone and
me only insofar as it had been the focus of group
organization.

Along's interpretation of his own dream had furnished
the necessary enthusiasm which had persuaded the
others to go along with him. Having taken this responsibility and accomplished a catch. *Along* was
more firmly established as an authority on hunting.
(Stewart, 1947, p. 106)

It becomes much simpler to show the relationship between
community and dreams this way. Instead of a magical dream
by a big hunter we simply have *Along* having a dream. He
talked about it with his friends and some decided to go hunting
with him because they liked it. Those among the community
who were busy with other things did not join the hunt. The
presentation by *Along* was what carried authority in the community. The dream became meaningful only when, by con-
census, they followed him and lived out the dream.

PA BOT'S TRANCE—A SONG

The Senoi dream trance rituals seem larger than life in these writings. But when examined closely, they become simple statements about their lives.

> *Pa Bot* at Rening had originated a ceremony which was thought to honor and strengthen the spirit of Maize. He gives the following account of the manner in which his first *G Naak* dream arrived: I planted Maize, and when I planted it, the kernels died. Two days later I went to see, and there were no sprouts. I went away and planted again elsewhere. When I slept, an ear of maize, which changed into a young girl, said to me: "You are stupid, this soil is bad." She gave me a song which I still sing during the *G Naak*.

> *Return Muse for the day is dawning,*
> *I send back the Maize soul along the trail of the sunset,*
> *Our hearts are still, let us sit together.*

> . . . . By singing the song and performing the maize dance, *Bot* and his friends believed that they increased the status of the maize spirit in its world and strengthened seed for the future. (Stewart, 1947, p. 172)

In reviewing all the primary data that Stewart presents we were impressed by the naturalness of the Senoi. The dreams took on their real significance when lived out in a community. The consequences were everyday and immediate. Dreams and songs rarely outlived their initiators. The Senoi life and dreams were simply about people living and sharing their lives by expressing feelings.

WAKING VERSUS DREAMING

More interesting than the types of dreams that the Senoi had were the types of lives they lived. When people read about the Senoi they immediately begin hoping, "maybe I can learn to control my dreams." Such an emphasis misses the entire point of Senoi life. What the Senoi had was a way of living and helping each other in their lives, a way which was both fun and meaningful. These latter two words may seem to be strange bedfellows, but so are dreaming and waking. The Senoi tested the reality of their projections, both during the day and the night, and acted on their feeling impulses. What they achieved was not stranger than life, but an example of simple living.

During the last few years the Senoi have become the focal point of numerous popular books extolling the virtues of dreams. The books are popular nonfiction quite unrelated to the primary data reported by Stewart and Noone.

The result has been that the dream life of the Senoi has become more publicized than the community life of the Senoi. Their way of life produced a remarkable people and culture. The dream was just part of their life, the part on which they based their community of shared feelings.

> . . . . The absence of violent crime, armed conflict, and mental and physical diseases in their own society can only be explained on the basis of institutions which produce a high state of psychological integration and emotional maturity, along with social skills and attitudes which promote and create, rather than destructive, interpersonal relations. . . . They have arrived at this high state of social and physical cooperation and integration through the system of psychology which they discovered, invented and developed. . . . (Stewart in Tart, 1969, p. 160)

What seems so different about the Senoi is not that they shared their dreams but that they also shared their feelings. It was the Senoi's communal attitudes which shaped their functional and wise psychology. What we have been discussing is the Senoi as they were, and not as they are today. The primacy of their communal attitude is clearly shown when we see what happened to their dreams and their psychology after their community structure was disrupted following World War II. The effect of relocation was as bad for them as a similar disruption had been for the American Iroquois Indians.

In the late 1940s and 1950s, Senoi life was grossly disrupted. Communist rebellions at that time had reached deep into the jungles. The terrorists had involved some of the jungle people and in response the government relocated them where they could be kept under closer supervision. The first relocation was purely a military affair, resulting in a great loss of property and life which the Senoi "remembered with dread" (Stewart, 1947, p. 177).

The profound changes in the Senoi wrought by rebellion, relocation, and subsequent return to their homeland can only be estimated. They had been known for their non-violent ways.

> The Semai do not say, "Anger is bad." They say, "We do not get angry," and an obviously angry man will flatly deny his anger. The Semai do not say, "It is forbidden to hit people." They say, "We do not hit people. . . ." Similarly, although the often heard statement that "we never hit our children," is primarily lip service to the nonviolent image, people do not often hit their children and almost never administer the kind of beating that is routine in some sectors of Euro-American society. A person should never hit a child because, people say, "How would you feel if it died?" (Dentan, 1968, pp. 55–56, 58)

These statements must be contrasted with the following one:

Many people who knew the Semai insisted that such an unwarlike people could never make good soldiers. Interestingly enough, they were wrong. Communist terrorists had killed the kinsmen of some of the Semai counterinsurgency troops. Taken out of their non-violent society and ordered to kill, they seem to have been swept up in a sort of insanity which they call "blood drunkenness." A typical veteran story runs like this. "We killed, killed, killed. The Malays would stop and go through people's pockets and take their watches and money. We do not think of watches or money. We thought only of killing." (Dentan, 1968, pp. 58-59)

What happened? As the Senoi community and way of life was broken, so was their cultural heritage. A principle of non-violence becomes a bizarre practice in time of war. It is interesting that war left them unharmed, but relocation because of the communist insurgency deprived them of one of the most remarkable features of their culture. Even their dream practices were perverted. Pat Noone, the British anthropologist who introduced Stewart to the Senoi, was killed by one of them. His murder occurred after their culture had been disrupted so that the communal sharing of dreams was no longer being practiced.

I asked him why he had done this terrible thing. He said he dreamed he must. I said, "Your dreams are false. You killed our Tata because you wanted his wife. You killed him because he has no relatives in the jungle to avenge him. But when the white men come back they will kill you for this deed." (Richard Noone with Dennis Holman, *In Search of the Dream People*, 1972, p. 183)

What was lacking in Noone's murderer's dream was community. Previously, anti-social action in dreams had been interpreted as illusion. Stewart describes numerous examples of the group interpreting dreams and coming to a group consensus. That was what was to be lived out of the dream. When the dream is not lived out within a community, the "dream people" lose their special power.

The postwar Senoi returned to their tribal and nonviolent way of life generally, but the deterioration of their culture had begun. With the introduction of money via cash crops, the need for communal sharing began to lessen. When the society was broken down, the dream practices which helped cohere and direct the society were no longer able to bring it together. What happened to the Senoi gives dramatic proof that community comes first, and dream practices follow to give the community its sophistication.

7

A MODERN DREAMER COMMUNITY

More than anything, it would be our wish that we had found some new and exotic therapy that would help us make our own life and the lives of our patients a paradise. That is not the case. What we have found is something that goes beyond therapy and the exotic. We found that as we pushed Feeling Therapy to its limits, the limits gave way and what we thought to be a therapy was an opening to life . . . toward entirely new ways of living. (*Going Sane,* 1975, p. 411)

. . . It was the result, he was certain, of a novel experiment he had undertaken with his friends. They too are psychologists and they live together, work together and practice on each other. . . . Binder calls the move a return to the tribal way of life . . . (Betty Liddick, *The Los Angeles Times,* Sunday, June 13, 1976)

If it had been possible for the Senoi to come and visit our community, we do not think that they would have found it strange. Without speaking our language, they would have understood much of what we do. Rather than having been perplexed by a technological lifestyle, they would have noticed the community lifetime. They would probably have focused not on our differences, but on what our two communities had in common.

FROM THERAPY TO COMMUNITY

It would be a mistake to read this chapter and come away with the idea that to work with dreams transformatively you need to go to dream groups and undergo intensive psychotherapy. These are techniques of no more value than Senoi dream trances, dances, and visions. We share with the Senoi one important fact of living: the attitude of making the private public. We live with this attitude as the primary feature of our lives.

The sharing of internal events is important to us. The threshold of privacy in our community has been lowered to accommodate the expression of feelings, thoughts, and dreams. It is the physical manifestation of the theory and history we have presented to this point.

Like our theory, our community gradually formed, not as an adjunct to our therapy but out of our basic needs. As the therapy was pushed to its limits, the limits gave way to something greater—a new psychological community. And as we developed community our dreams changed. The conversion of private to public life allowed the transformative dream to supplant the compensatory dream in the lives of the community members. From the development of transformative dreaming we were able to modify and expand our therapeutic structure and practice. Community came first, and our dream practices followed.

> Today thirteen of them—psychologists, counselors, one psychiatrist and their mates—live in a row of four houses. . . . and are enclosed by one natural wood fence so that dogs can run free and children play. . . . (Betty Liddick, June 13, 1976)

Presently more than three hundred people are involved in our community, over half living within a three block radius.

At the center of this circle is the "compound" where the founding members of the community reside. A heavily traveled path runs in front of the compound separating it from other houses that face it in the typical American city fashion. A redwood fence and thick hedge further define the core of the village forming a large rectangle more than half a block long. Within these confines four houses sit together, unbound by any external divisions. Rose bushes, shrubbery and fences have been removed and a grassy field substituted. Three of the houses are typical half-century old woodframes, with large porches and gently sloping shingle roofs. The fourth house is made of stucco and is capped by red tile, a facsimile of the dwellings native to the region.

The back yards all open together forming a large field containing an orchard, basketball court, playing area and swimming pool. This large area is shared with and enclosed by the four other homes that face the rear of the compound from the street that runs behind. Since they, too, are connected by a large fence, the eight houses encircle an enclosed courtyard.

The houses have been opened to each other. Intervening fences were removed and doors and windows added. Wooden decks and runways were constructed to connect each house and facilitate contact between them. These changes were undertaken step-by-step until the compound achieved a form that we later realized would be more in accord with what the Senoi would find familiar.

It is interesting to note that the average home opens to the street in front, where endless streams of strangers drive or walk by in the course of the day. Most people do not find it strange to purchase a home among other homes inhabited by strangers. They live many years in a neighborhood without sharing anything of substance other than an occasional greeting. The Senoi would find this feature of American life totally perplexing. How could a people build their *saka* with all the huts facing the wrong direction, and then compound the error by allowing strangers to travel through their midst and further divide them with well-traveled paths?

Perhaps we have all been motivated by the fear of a loss of privacy. It was not without trepidation that our first walls were removed. We were afraid that "something" would be taken away by this loss of privacy. When we began to focus on what would be gained by sharing time together the fears fell away. With each step we had to deal with this intrusion of old images upon our present lives. As our feelings expanded so did our ability to live in a community. Our community slowly developed over eight years, slowly unraveling and dealing with the knots and ties that came from our old pictures of how we should live.

The houses were opened inside as well, to match the open spaces that formed outside in the yards. Large living-dining-cooking rooms became the focus for visiting, sharing and working together, similar in function to the communal long houses of the Iroquois and the Senoi. These newly developing structures facilitated our helping each other in a natural way during the course of the day.

We began our community with the knowledge that we needed contact, and that we could help each other achieve it. The structures emerged from this belief. We could have had a community in a rural setting, or in the city. What was essential was not the location but its capabilities — how it met our needs as its members. Time and space were set aside in our compound for sharing. Our system of psychology was not outside of the way we lived — it *was* the way we lived.

GROUP LEADERSHIP

We share with the Senoi the concept and practice of group leadership. We have no written code or set of laws, but it is a fact that those patients and therapists who have had the most experience seem to maintain the most influence. As the founders of our community, we have given and received the most help, and have shared our dreams and feelings over the longest periods. The leadership of the community falls to us, but not to one man or one director or one theoretician. There is no "head man," and everyone exercises authority.

> . . . therapeutic systems are usually limited by the burden of a single founder who tries to make a structure for others but does not fully and equally participate in it himself. This lack of therapy and participation by the founder leads to theoretical and practical rigidities. The founder's own disordered or psychotic idiosyncracies cannot be withdrawn from the system; instead they become rationalized within the structure of the therapy. (*Going Sane,* 1975, p. 321)

Decisions are not carried out by edict or doctrinal compliance, but through the mutuality of feeling. Often one founder or community member can influence the others through the powerful appeal to their feelings. Anything that feels incomplete is not acted upon until it feels complete; leadership is continually tested and supported.

As with the Senoi, the emphasis should not be on the fact that there are founders who rule the community, but on the fact of group leadership. Obviously we do not make personal decisions for our patients. But the overall direction of the therapeutic community is in the collective hands of its oldest members. Newer members are helped to establish their own community within the community, their own circle of influence and rotating leadership. Just as we sought each other's help, we show them how this process can work for them, so that they begin to acquire the skills of being both people who can accept aid, and people who can give it.

This fact of ascending leadership works for the community on both a personal and a general level. As a patient begins to act as a *co-therapist* for his or her friends, that person begins to change his or her own image from that of being a patient to being a friend. This, in turn, opens important new areas of personal development and helps to expand the person's range of feeling and action. The patient is responsible to him- or herself, and to others; and with this expansion of feeling and feeling authority comes personal transformation. Increased responsibility also leads to community transformation, which adds to the community and helps it sustain each individual.

TRANSLATIONS

To help understand our community, we want to make a number of translations as we did with the Senoi. Many readers who are interested in dreams and dream theory may not be interested in reading about "therapeutic intervention," "patient," "therapist," or "therapeutic community." But it is necessary to translate a number of terms that have to do with our experiences in psychotherapy. It is easy to get lost in the technical or theoretical aspects of a psychotherapy and ignore the real human consequences of these aspects. In translating these terms we may correct some misleading impressions and help relate the way we live to the way we theorize about dreams.

> **Therapeutic community.** A feeling community must be capable of two essential functions: first, it must cope with the recurrent bouts of insanity of its members and, second, it must extend and support the feeling openness that people acquire as they return to sanity. The first capability is therapeutic and the second is transformative. One is not enough without the other for they are complementary. We realized that being a patient was therapeutic but not transformative, and we began to act on our needs

for something more than a therapy session or a therapy. (*Going Sane,* 1975, p. 340)

A therapeutic community is not the place where we live our lives. It is the way we live. It seems ironic to us that the concept of a community existing to help and heal connotes something restrictive rather than expansive. A translation becomes necessary to counter the negative beliefs that people have about community.

Some see it as limited and restrictive, and terrifying to join. On the other hand, others think it an expanding, feelingful, loving group of people having a wonderful life, sharing work and play. Of course both points of view are beliefs. In actuality we are a group of people living our lives together fully aware of how we are spending our time.

What most people overlook is that they already live in a form of community, one which may be based on ethnic, professional or geographical limits. Everyone takes part in a community, and the roles individuals play is not determined by where they live as much as by how they live and how much sharing of feeling takes place. Since, as is often the case, most people do not allow themselves to evaluate and feel the consequences of their way of living, they live in unintentional communities. Our community differs mainly in that it is an intentional one.

It is necessary for a community to be intentional, for time to be spent experiencing the how of community life, thus allowing the two functions of the therapeutic community as we described it in *Going Sane* to be fulfilled. First, the increased awareness of the members allows them to interact and respond to the struggles people make to adjust to life from the disordering patterns of childhood. These interactions are therapeutic in the formal sense and often take place in the therapy sessions. But instead of the help being administered by a professional stranger with little firsthand experiencing of the person's lifestyle, it is given by a friend or peer who sees and knows that individual in a more complete manner.

The interactions are therapeutic in the informal sense as well, since this kind of contact exceeds the bounds of the therapy session both in time and place. Co-therapists discuss cases with each other and can react appropriately as patients apply or misapply what they have learned in each session.

Second, the community exists to support and extend the feeling openness that is achieved in the intense therapy sessions through friends interested in promoting feeling contact with each other. This community function is transformative and complements the therapeutic structure of our intentional community.

The Patient. It is necessary to redefine "patient." If two people are together in a room and a therapeutic session is taking place, the patient is the one receiving help. For experienced patients the term has a transient quality about it, since they are aware the roles can be reversed.

The Therapist. A label for the person who is helping.

Therapeutic Intervention. Some people are hesitant about undergoing therapeutic intervention, or even therapy. We understand it to mean the establishment of contact.[1] When a person expresses a complete feeling he makes contact both with himself and with others. Contact — through the expression of complete feelings flowing out to those around us — is what we attempt to accomplish in our therapeutic interventions. We interfere directly in someone's disordering pattern to establish contact.

Just as were the Senoi, so are we concerned with the affective and dreamer education of our members. It is a form of re-education, for we learned that the disordering or censoring process was secondary, and we became concerned about reintroducing the primary impulse to express feelings completely and openly. To re-educate dreamers, we help them learn to share dreams and feelings as part of the structure of the therapy. The therapeutic process remains the same. In the following pages we will introduce a therapeutic structure that expands as the patient expands his or her own feeling expressiveness.

The Initiation. Imagine what it would be like to join, even for a brief time, a tribe of the Temiar Senoi in Malaysia's Northern Perak. You could watch and observe them living their dreams and dancing their lives, but you would not experience their way of life by so doing. To do more than watch would require an intense initial effort both on your part and by the tribe.

You could not do it alone. You would not know what to do or when to do it. Some warrior of the tribe would have to want to help you join, and help you take part. He would have to contact you on the edge of the council fire, and invite you in. And as you got to know and trust him, you would begin to share your first dream. He would create a ritual dance just for you, based on the community that you two had just established, as well as on the particular ways you react to that community. This ritual would constantly change and finally cease to be a ritual at all.

You thought there would be a ritual. You would come to the tribe expecting an initiation. And only after a while would you begin to realize that the ritual really didn't exist—that there was really only you, your feelings and your warrior.

At first the rituals seemed done *to* you and that was what you wanted. Gradually, as the intensity of the first few months wore away your life-learned process of disordering, and slowly turned you toward expression and transformation, you would begin to experience the rituals as your own creation. No longer would things be done to you. There would just be your feelings and your experience.

When a person enters our community he demands to be

a patient, at least at the beginning, and we allow it because it is a natural and good first step. Then he chooses to begin to share, a choice that he will have to repeat over and over. The more natural this choice becomes for him, the less need he will have to call himself a patient. The ritual of patient and therapist, early in the therapy, seems necessary. Then, trusting the therapist warrior, he will allow himself to follow the experience of his own dreams and begin the journey of transformation. Without this trust and contact the journey is impossible.

During this early initiation phase, the patient will have intensive open-ended periods of time with his therapist for two months. He will share his dreams, feelings, images and defenses in periods of time from thirty minutes to three hours. It is so intense a process that the therapist is unable to initiate more than one person at a time into the community. When he is not attending the individual sessions, the patient will spend six to ten hours in groups and other therapy-related activities. For the Senoi, participation in the community does not consist of isolated activities. The initiate is involved continuously. So, too, is our patient as he prepares to enter his dream community.

The initial structure of the therapeutic community is based on establishing contact between the therapist and the patient, and on allowing it to expand into a tentative and frightening new community of initiates. Then, as progress is made, the structure changes again to meet the needs of the patient.

The Meeting. The therapist is part of a community of therapists, all working simultaneously, and there may be from six to twelve initiates at any time. The initiate is immediately part of a group who have something remarkable in common — they are undergoing change in their lives. They form an experimental community and they begin to meet in their own dream group.

Just as the Senoi child first presents his dream to his

parents, the new patient presents his dream to his therapist. As the child matures he is helped to take responsibility for his thoughts and dreams by verbalizing them in a larger group. So, too, is the new patient helped to talk and share his dreams and feeling with his group members. This initial group represents the first small community from which the patient will learn and to which he will contribute. The power and influence of this community within a community will grow as each member expands his or her power of expression, clarity, feeling and role, growing in confidence as the patient exercises personal influence within the safer confines of this first dream group.

The individual members of the group begin to transform their lives from holding in to expressing under the guidance of a therapist. Since individual contact with the original therapist also continues, although in a less intense manner, the group becomes a place to live out the insights and feelings that emerged from this more private contact. In this way both the group and the individual patient mature. As responsibility for feelings and thoughts increases, friendship begins to replace therapeutic structure.

The Meeting Intensifies. As the young Senoi becomes mature enough to share his big dream with the rest of the tribe fully, so does the patient become experienced enough to begin taking a more active role in the community. Eventually he becomes familiar with both his own dream processes and those of his friends. As he is able to express rather than repress what he sees and feels, he is able to expand his range of influence even more. He begins to accept help, not merely from a therapist, but from his peers, and is called on to administer such help to his friends. He is not just changing as part of an exercise, but is instrumental in his own change. The original structure of patient and therapist begins to be broken down into friends helping each other with their dreams so that each can enjoy the intense feeling lives within. It is not unusual for older members of the community to regard their dream groups in the same manner as a Senoi regards his *saka*.

Revolving Authority. No dream community can be complete unless all members are involved as both dream tellers and dream dancers. People need to help and be helped in order to sustain a transformative community. Without revolving authority the community dies. Once this authority is firmly established, the structure of the therapeutic community expands to fit the lives the members lead. It is not limited to specific times and places, but is present whenever group members and friends are present. In this way the two requirements of the therapeutic community are met. The insanity of disordering is opposed whenever it is necessary and friends allow each other to live out their newfound feeling. As this occurs, the person who came to the tribe as patient takes full part in all aspects of the community. He becomes "one of us."

PAUL'S WEEK

The following shows what one week in the life of "one of us" — a trainee therapist in Functional Therapy—is like, the type of life he leads and the kinds of dreams he dreams. It shows how he is constantly checking on his feelings, and using his awareness of his waking and dream life to change the way he lives. He is not a passive victim of the events that make up his life. It is comparable to *Along's* Senoi hunting trip of the last chapter.

Session: Saturday Morning. I began the session just talking about anything that came into my mind. I had wanted to buy a Willy Jeep that week, and was sad that it had been sold. In fact, I knew I couldn't afford to buy it, but I wanted it anyway. When I want—I get quiet and hold myself back. R. had me stand up and follow J. around with my back leading the way. J. was telling me to just follow his voice and I just kept following blindly. I liked J. talking to me, and just saying, "Follow me." I began to cry, but after a while I even stopped that and just followed J.'s voice, feeling my body begin shaking. I felt a big area in my back, my stomach began to tense up, and I began to choke with feelings. R. came by and said to just let the uncontrollable feelings emerge and not to choke them off. I was feeling myself give in to someone. My jaw let go and hung down on my chest. I gave in more and more into them calling me — and into my own feeling. I started shaking and moving, letting go of the controls. Then R. came over and eased me down into J.'s arms. I wept with my whole body, my whole chest and back, deeper than I had ever wept in my life. I looked at J. and saw his face. I was not afraid or distant. He looked clear. I could see his sadness and I felt totally clear and alive, like I had connected up my body from the top to the bottom.

Waking: Saturday. I left the session and played music that afternoon with J. and R. I also watched the UCLA-USC football game with R. and had a great time. I roared like I never had before. Then I rested, and my wife P. and I had dinner. I was having real fun. I saw a poor movie and came home and went to sleep, feeling good and very tired.

Dream: Saturday Night. *Me bicycling down the street, a fugitive, running along with Honey, my dog. I bicycle along and this little boy, my little boy, is right beside me, talking to me, telling me which way to go, how to get away. I see my sister, Karen, and she is telling me to stay. I say, "No," to her. I go to this abandoned barn and say goodbye to my son. Even though I am leaving him we are happy because*

*I will be free. Karen does not want to lose me. I try
to make it through this barn to the other side where
I will be safe, and no one will find my tracks. I remember one door is so small I had to know how to
undo the little windows to crawl through. Karen was
below yelling at me. She fell through the floor and
came out a drain on the outside. She struggled fran-
tically in the water. I thought she died, but she lived
and I heard her say: "He is free—there it is . . . " I
saw a light and the free land. I was happy . . . I
didn't know which way to jump to get there myself—
down my way or hers. I had to jump down and get
through a fence before I was free. I felt afraid, but
I wanted to move.*

Summary: Saturday's Child. His dream comes from his
community experience. He has therapy in the morning and
then does various things in the afternoon. The people who help
him in the morning are the friends he sees in the afternoon.
This gives him a "new present" in the session, and new ways
of more fully expressing himself in the afternoon. He continues his openness into the afternoon, and the transition is
natural and easy, since he is with the same people who have
just helped him.

This new present enables him to have a dream with elements of power. In many ways there are fantastic things happening. We can interpret that the little boy is equal to a Senoi
spirit. It closely parallels what he must face in his life—allowing
himself the freedom to be smaller. He is smaller not because
he is expressing childish feelings, but because, as an adult, he
needs help and is finally able to take it from his community
members. He went on to experience symbolically in his dream
what he felt as a child—fear, confusion, and finally a way out.

The defenses that he worked with in the morning session
were broken sufficiently so that he was free to begin to break

the defenses at their origins in the past. Since this way of trusting is so new to him, he is not able to complete the movement necessary to take him to freedom. He is close enough to see where he must go. And he is aware enough to realize that he must choose and that ultimately he is responsible for the movement that will free him.

It is interesting to view the session during the morning as equal to the Senoi trance. A time has been set aside, he enlists his friends' help, they dance the feeling together, and he emerges with a new experience of himself. He tests this experience out during the day, and that night discovers a new feeling and a new vision. The relationship between the trance and dreams becomes much clearer.

> **Waking: Sunday.** I went to work and told R. my dream. He laughed. He looked tired. When I worked, I worked out of my dream. Afterward, we all had lunch together. I told K. that I was afraid of losing what I had and she and D. told me that it was impossible to lose what is already mine. That night I worked a group with L. and really enjoyed myself. I felt totally close to L., confident in myself that I was a therapist, that I was working, that I had friends . . . I felt great when I went to bed. In the middle of the night I awakened and P. and I began to make love. As I got more and more excited, I stopped expressing my feelings, and I began to think more and more, literally making up images to scare myself more. I got so afraid I would not talk to P. and instead I pushed her away. Just before I went to sleep I told her I was sorry for getting hard, but that I was afraid.

> **Dream: Sunday Night.** *In my dream I saw a picture of my body. I saw it closing in, and I knew that if I did not talk, my rib cage would pull in on itself.*

Summary: Sunday's Shaman. The patient is faced with living out his new feeling. When he doesn't, he has a dream with shamanistic qualities. It tells him explicitly what will happen to him — he will close down. It is a healing dream and if he is to remain healthy he must live out its instruction: "Talk!"

Waking: Monday. I went to Whittier to talk to my supervisor for field work. I enjoyed talking with her, although I felt afraid and distrusting from the night before. Before I left for the appointment I talked to P. and asked her if she was angry. She pushed me away although she said, "No." When I got back she was cold and told me she did not want to stay with me anymore. I knew she was just hurt, but I couldn't stop her from lashing out at me. I tried talking, but she continued. I pulled away and told her I didn't want to be with her either (though inside I knew we would be back together tomorrow). I slept alone that night, twisted up inside, blaming her and feeling lonely.

Dream: Monday Night. *I dreamed that I put P. in a room separate from me because I didn't feel safe with her anymore. She was trying to hurt me and I felt lonely and frightened.*

Summary: Monday's Paranoia. In this dream he is giving up what he knows from Saturday's session and experience. Instead of following the healing direction of his session and dreams, he allows himself to blame his wife. His dream immediately correlates with his day's activity. Forgetting that trusting is totally his choice and responsibility, he is lost in the symbolism of frightening pictures and enemies. His dream is controlling him now, and he is a victim of its pictures.

Waking: Tuesday. P. and I talked and I started to soften a little. I called K. and talked to her for a long time and could begin to feel myself with her. I went to school to take my final exams. I came home and spent the evening with R. and K. I felt lonely and sick inside for getting twisted up, and it was nice to be with my friends with no insanity between us. I stayed until late, not really wanting to go at all.

Dream: Tuesday Night. *I dreamed that R. and W. were teaching me how to use the "fire" inside of me.*

Summary: Tuesday's Man. By Tuesday, Paul has begun to use his community. He is talking and allowing himself to escape from the old pictures once again. He is able to receive help and, so, live from the level of feeling that is possible for him. Two special authorities with whom he has contact are incorporated in his dream and teach him how to use his "fire."[2]

Waking: Wednesday. I spent the day with P. shopping and talking. During a meeting with D. about a coming lecture, I talked to him about how I felt, that if I exposed how afraid I was to lecture he would not let me lecture . . . D. talked to me and told me it was okay to be afraid and that I would certainly be able to lecture. P. and I slept together that night and really enjoyed each other. We talked a lot.

Dream: Wednesday Night. *Dreams about R. telling me about power. Me knowing power. In one dream, I was taking an exam. I was tense. It was some qualifying examination. I finished it fast. I knew I was smarter than all the others. I also dreamed about being with this guy and going to his house. He tried to sell me everything, seeing his family, all strange people. I don't want to be a victim of a strange world.*

Summary: Wednesday's Victor. Paul has taken a deeper move into the community. The revolving authority has shifted as he seeks and gets more contact and help from D. His personal relationship with P. has changed as he feels close to himself, and now is able to be with her. Wednesday night he is ready for a prospective dream.

This dream is prospective in that he feels his own natural intelligence. He has been given advice from his dream teachers on how to use his fire and now his power. He applies his power in the dream in a very practical and simple way—an exam in school. He is beginning to be who he really is, instead of the self-doubting and self-deprecating person he had been brought up to be. He had allowed D. to interfere in his life, to allow him to express the fears so that they could be dealt with rather than destroy him secretly from within.

Waking: Thursday. I was with E. and N., and D. came to the door. He looked tormented. He shouted, "Open the door!" and I said, "No." He got even more angry and I became frightened. I knew the door was not locked, but was simply stuck, but he was too upset to even try. I made fun of him just to keep talking and he finally got the door open. I felt his rage as he walked by and swore at me. I wanted to attack him, but I knew from the week before where this would lead me, how it feels to get engaged in a fight, so I stopped. I left still thinking of how to hurt D. Not wanting to be twisted inside, I went home and talked to A. about how I had gotten frightened. For a moment A. was with me and I felt how frightened and unsteady I was. Then he began telling me what I should do. I began to feel bad again and told him. Then J. came in and then they both told me that I should talk to D. and straighten it out.

Dream: Thursday Night. *I was getting ready to run this big group, taking notes on different people. Then I was at a park waiting with everyone until*

*group. This big girl kept walking by and I wanted
to make love with her. I felt that same way I felt as
a kid. She led me to a parking lot and I knew she had
friends that would hurt me, so I left. R. was there.
He said that I did not have to lead the group, that
I could be a patient. I was glad. We got in the car
and D. was sitting next to me. All my friends were
in the car. D. got everyone to help him because he
was feeling so bad. I stopped and said, "You are
making us help you. You are not my friend. I came
to see you two weeks ago and you talked to me, and
now you hurt me. You did not take care of yourself.
You hurt me and now I am alone with you."*

Summary: Thursday's Loner. He is still alone and blaming others in his dream. He has not gotten the support he needs from his community. He has lost much of what he had before. He needs responses rather than advice so that he can become aware of how he gives up his own feeling by having thoughts about others. This was clear in the first part of the dream in which he stops his sexual feeling by a false clarity, much the same way he stopped his sexual feelings with his wife by thinking and not expressing some nights before. He is aware in the dream that he needs to enlist the help of his dream teachers, and this allows the dream to shift. He is clear and lucid, but again his own feeling is withheld by having thoughts about D. He now needs to live out the dream in waking and begin to talk to D., showing his feeling rather than his insights.

Waking: Friday. I spent the day with K. and R. just resting. I worked on the yard a bit. D. called on R. and I stopped him and talked to him. I told him I was lonely and that he hurt me. For a little while he fought back, but he later said he had been feeling really mixed-up and hard, and that he did not want to hurt me. I felt much better after talking to him.

Dream: Friday Night. *Many dreams. One long one that stands out is where I am at this retreat and we are running and playing and there are three bears right above me. We run to safety but the bears were not mean. We play. Later a lion comes down and we play fear games about the lion and look around and there are many hunters looking to kill the lion. I am sad and scared when I see that. Then R. tells me, "You are starting to open up now. You are afraid to get involved with a man on a new level. It seems like a lot to feel, but it is just your loneliness."*

Summary: Friday's Seer. The dream of Friday night is totally involved with Paul's battle for clarity. In the first part of the dream he is able to play with the bears after becoming aware that the bears were not enemies. This represents a real clarity and a subsequent change of role, from escaping to playing. In the second part of the dream he is able to play with his own fear, not taking it seriously. He is not subject to his false clarity. He is afraid and sad when he sees the result of his fears — hunters killing the lion out of fear.

The third part of the dream restates the previous action of the dream as the feeling is maintained. The dream is wonderfully clear and explicit, telling him both what to do and what he is actually feeling. The dream needs no further interpretation. What is called for is action based on the clarity. He needs to talk to D. and to others from within, about his own feelings. Otherwise the distance he maintains from others, symbolized by his struggle with D., will continue, and he will remain afraid and alone. In this respect the dream is similar to his dream the night before. The dream processes will not let him ignore what he needs to do, nor will his feeling change until he takes effective action.

Waking: Saturday. I rested and later worked with L. I did not trust him. I was worried again about how he was going to reprimand me. I did not feel good in group, and L. and I talked after. Some of the time I felt good about my work and made contact, but that recurring insanity with L. disturbed me.

Dream: Saturday Night. *L. and I were at a country place and I wanted a candy bar. L. lent me the money. I began talking to him about last night's group. I told him how I thought he was too concerned with minor things, and overlooked feelings. I told him that he was criticizing me too much, and was not simply "with me." Then I started crying about how afraid I was to work with him, to "follow" him, to allow him the power of helping me. I cried and showed him how afraid I was. I looked up and he was crying too. I asked him if I made him sad. He said, "I have feelings like that, too. You don't make me sad." Then J. came in and talked softly to both of us. I felt awkward, but like I was part of a group in change.*

Summary: Saturday's Senoi. This dream shows the community at work, as he is adding more dream teachers. In the Senoi sense he is gaining power with each additional dream teacher. He is again living out of a deeper level of feeling, and is free to feel more directly in the dream. He is transforming, becoming someone more able to express his own feelings. He ends the dream with a lucid knowing that he is part of a group in change. This is a significant realization of his own changing, and of being "one of us."

Session: Sunday Morning. I began uncertain of how I felt. I told K. about my thoughts about L. K. told me to simply talk to him more often and not to work with him unless I was close to him. She helped me with my chest, helping me to stay sad and breathe deeply. At the end of the session I just held on to her, telling her, "I need you, I'm going away." I kept repeating that and feeling more and more my deep loneliness. I called to her from a place inside of me that I had never called from before. I felt close to her, and after the session, I went to L.'s house, and we talked and got close.

This concludes Paul's week in much the same manner as Along concluded his hunting trip, and Pa Bot his song. The week was noteworthy because of its naturalness. We see more than big dreams. We see natural lives and natural acts. The dream's importance did not outlive the dreamer and his day. The consequences were both everyday and immediate.

Paul had finally come full circle, finally integrating the first session in which he had simply followed and begun to trust others at a deeper level than he had before. His struggles to accept his own feelings over his projections and insights about others were remarkably parallel in his waking and dream lives. The community support during the day allowed more and more expression and movement to take place in his dreams. And after he awoke each day, he had a community on which to test his new movements and new expressions. His life is both full and simple.

The story of Paul's week allows us to realize that even the very best psychotherapeutic experience, of one very willing patient with one very skilled and feelingful therapist, is still inadequate to sustain transformative dreaming and a transformative way of living. For Paul it took much more. Nevertheless, in our culture, people pay therapists to listen to them and help them — to be their friends. And once they "get well" they are supposed to be able to return home to their own communities.

Whenever a patient begins seeing a therapist of any kind, from bioenergetics to psychoanalysis, he or she first enters a structured environment. The structure of the therapy may be one particular room at one particular time. In the beginning this limited and rigid structure allows for movement and expression. Contact ensues because this one hour, if only one hour a week, still exceeds what the patient was able or willing to do in his or her life outside that room.

When that contact is established there exists a small community of two, complete for that instant of time and place. Then that contact process needs to move into the rest of the patient's life. If the therapy is successful, and the patient becomes more expressive and complete, the boundaries of time and place must be expanded to allow the patient to live from this greater completeness. If the therapeutic structure remains the same, the therapeutic process becomes limited and symbolic.

> Every new therapeutic orientation tries to offer a better technique or a better theory, but almost no attention is given to the structure that must exist if the techniques of theories are to be realized. *Therapeutic structure is the most neglected component of therapeutic effectiveness.* (*Going Sane*, 1975, p. 321)

What is generally true of psychotherapeutic theories is also true for dream theories. The different ways of exchanging dreams are neglected. If the way of exchanging is neglected then the way the dreamer behaves in the dream will also be neglected. The focus will be on content. In place of dream communities we have dream theories and research about dreams. But theories and research mean nothing for individual dreamers unless the insight they give can be put into practice. It is the structure of a dream community that limits what can be dreamed, and how dreams can be changed.

ADVICE FOR SOLO DREAMERS

We recognize that very few people who read this book will have available to them a community in which they can fully share their dreams, feelings and lives. If such communities were widely available then the normative dream in our society would be the transformative dream, not the symbolic dream.

You must practically ask yourself, therefore, "What can I do on my own?" And the best answer to that is: "Take steps now so that you don't stay on your own, in your dreams or in your life."

We would advise you first of all — to notice who is in your dreams and notice how you emotionally respond to them. If you dream of strangers and not about the people you live and work and play with, then you are not functioning with your friends at a very high emotional level.

The second piece of advice is to share your dreams with the people you see often. Even if you are not now emotionally close with these people, by sharing dreams you will soon increase your closeness. But remember, just share your dreams and invite them to share theirs. Do not interpretively analyze or functionally analyze the dreams.

By taking these first steps you will be moving toward the creation of your own dreamer community.

For more steps we suggest that you consult our manual on using dreams, *The Dream Makers,* and go through the guided twenty-one day program with one or more other people.

8

TRANSFORMATION IN THERAPY: AN EXAMPLE

> Helene Deutsch, on the other hand, seemed to me very beautiful and cold. Once I gave her a present and instead of a "thank you" I got an interpretation in return. (Perls, *In and Out the Garbage Pail,* 1969)

In musing on his early days of training in Vienna in 1927, Fritz Perls told the anecdote above about one of his supervisors, Helene Deutsch. This episode between Perls and Deutsch shows, far better than any theoretical treatise, the role of interpretation in their relationship. In these next chapters, we will use transcripts to show the role of transformation in our relationships.

We began this book by calling for a re-acknowledgment of the importance of the affective drive—the drive to create contact through feeling expression. We theorized that people become disordered when cognitive functions overwhelm affect. For many people, a disordered lifestyle is like a dream—symbolic, distorted by images and unpleasant. We said that we stress feeling processes during the day in order to achieve transformation. We now want to show the theory in clinical practice in its most simple and human form.

Content and content analysis have had the same over-emphasis in clinical practice that they have had in dream research. We are shifting that emphasis in our clinical work. In working with feelings generated in waking and dreaming, we emphasize five processes[1] — role, expression, feeling, clarity, and contact. More than a means of describing dream dynamics or studying changes in dreams, they have a direct clinical application.

We do not primarily work with dreams or a person's feeling. We work with *the way* that person tells us about them. We observe *how* the role he or she plays aids the expression. We involve ourselves with *the way* he feels. And we listen to and support the insights and awareness that result from feeling.

We believe that *therapy sessions can be compared to transformative dreams.* In sessions there are movements from symbolic modes of expression to direct expression, from confusion to clear meanings about a person's life. The emotional coherence of the session or the dream is what is important.

THE FOUR PHASES IN THE CYCLE OF FEELING

The following transcript[2] of a therapy session contains the four phases in the cycle of feeling that comprise a patient's affective education. First, he becomes aware of how he disorders his feeling. Second, he feels the effects of disordering on his life at that moment. Third, he rediscovers the origins for disordering in his past, and how the disordering pattern affected him in past moments. Finally, he learns to separate past and present, allowing him to live with more feeling and clarity.

STEP 1: IMAGE AWARENESS
This patient uses his role, expression, feeling and clarity against

himself to remain unaware of the way he images. Although his session takes place in the "safety" of the therapy room and he is an experienced patient and therapist, and in spite of the fact that he knows full expression has helped him many times before, he must experience his defenses before he is able to feel himself. He must first become aware of the way he images.

P: Oh . . . [*Sighing*] . . . I don't really feel so bad now. It's just I know something is going on in the background, about me. Something going on . . .

These opening lines sound very much like what Hall and others report as the background feeling of most dreams — a general uneasiness and passivity. There is no self-awareness.

P: Like I don't even know what I'm feeling bad about . . . I just know that after my patient this morning I was really shaking, really shaking. Like I don't have much feeling about F. I think he'll be back Monday as dead as ever and I'll do something else with him.

T: What about the feeling *you* had, inside *you,* working with F. this morning, when it was over?

P: Well, I was, uh, shaking . . . I was just shaking, because I'd really gotten angry at him, really yelled and really pushed him and hit him with those bataca things . . . you know, nothing happened from that. I didn't really have feelings about that so much, ah, I have more . . . things like what we talked about last night were really important to me and I just kept thinking today I want to lay down, you know, without feeling real bad . . .

T: Well, just when I saw you sitting in the staff room . . .

P: Uh-huh . . .

T: You know, you looked like you had a lot of feeling right then . . . you know, you don't have to have feelings about F. I want you to talk about the feeling you have about yourself.

If you allow yourself the freedom in functional analysis of not concentrating on the content but on process, we see that the patient is not feeling completely. His feelings are being filtered through the processes of disordering. He appears to know something about himself. He knows which feelings are important and which are not. The ensuing transcript will show his apparent clarity to be completely false.

The general area of feeling is apparent. The patient indicates the precipitating event in the present, but is not yet focused in on it. He is very much like the dreamer who is more involved in an event in a dream than with his own feelings during that event. He had gotten angry at his patient that morning. He repeats the dialogue he had used, but he was really talking more about his patient than about himself. The therapist brings the emphasis back to him, what *he* is feeling.

P: [*Yelling*] Well, do something. What do you want to do? And I was really coming out at him . . . I hit him a few times on the legs with that thing (bataca) . . . I didn't want to hit him on the head . . . I was afraid to . . . I got afraid . . . [*Crying*] . . . I got afraid . . . to . . . hit . . . I knew he could . . . he could . . . probably take me in a fight . . . and I was afraid he would hit me really hard . . . you know, if he put that thing down and came at me physically . . . and I got really scared [*Crying*] . . . You know I was doing it just for him . . . I just could not stand any more of his deadness . . . and I just rapped him on the legs a little bit.

The crying here is about feeling. The patient has an image which allows him to cry, a picture that is the product of his defenses. In his image, he is weak and unable to respond. He is crying about the reasons he is not free to express himself. He is literally crying from a false clarity ("I can't because") and a false role ("I don't"). It is a false feeling— a feeling *from* a defense, not a feeling *of* the defense. It is the difference between crying about "I cannot follow through" and "I am not following through."

The patient has reasons why he cannot allow himself full expression. As the therapist works with him, his drive to express is brought forward and his drive for cognition is reduced, so that the defensive reasons are experienced rather than believed and acted out.

In a dream there is a reason for both fear and the inability to express it. For example—"There was a gorilla coming after me but he was too big to fight." This reasonable objection tries to make incomplete expression seem comprehensible as it protects the symbolism in the dream. Until he faces the gorilla, the dreamer has no chance to transform the symbol. This patient protects his daytime symbolism in the same manner.

To help counter this protection, the therapist again helps him focus on what *he* was doing, on *his* own response, rather than on what the other person was doing.

> T: . . . Did you do what you wanted to do with him to help him? Or did you have to hold back?
>
> P: I held back . . . I held back . . . I did not, you know, I did not just swat and bash . . . swat and bash.
>
> T: How does that feel inside you when you hold back?

The feeling is now much clearer and the patient is closer to it. The therapist will begin to work with the patient's body to raise the intensity of the newly defined feeling — "holding back." By noticing what holding back does to him, he is going to feel "his image."

STEP 2: FEELING THE IMAGING

People usually awaken from dreams without having gone through the defenses that keep their feelings incomplete. What is missing in symbolic dreams is the crucial reversal of disordering. In Functional Therapy the therapist provides this movement. A reality is created in order to allow the patient to experience his defense as it is happening — the therapist provokes him, just as the therapist-patient had tried to mobilize his own patient's aggression in the morning. This is extremely difficult to do because no one really wants to evoke violent feelings in another person.

T: Get up . . . just get as physically violent as you feel . . . as you felt like with him.

P: With you?

T: Just hit me on the legs . . . just do it . . . just feel it in your body.

P: [*Hitting with batacas*] That scares me to do that . . . I don't . . .

T: [*Loud*] Just do it!

P: I don't want to hurt you.

T: Just do it . . . just feel that in you . . . Do it! . . . No, you are holding back. You are holding back right now.

P: I don't want to hurt you.

T: No . . . *you* feel that, and do it . . . *you* feel it . . . it is you you are worried about . . . I'll feel me.

P: [*Hitting harder*]

T: You are still holding back . . . Come on, harder, harder! You are still really constricted.

Just as it happened that morning, he is unable to "follow through" and move "for himself." He opposes his own action by holding back, represented on a physical level by muscular activity (a false role), and on a cognitive level by worries and fears (a false clarity).

The therapist will exaggerate the "holding back" to increase the patient's feeling awareness. As he talks, the patient provides information that allows the therapist to create a technique. This technique forces the patient to experience his defense vividly as a defense.

P: I held back . . . you're right . . . everything you're saying is right . . . you know, I held back because I was afraid he would hurt me . . . he is really angry inside . . . just really angry inside . . . I keep coming back to that being afraid of being hurt . . . the holding back . . . that shows up all the time. *Yesterday . . . I was talking about playing paddleball yesterday, and there is just a little bit when I hold back* . . . and it is little but it's there . . . just holding back a little bit so I will hit the ball but it won't go far enough or I will hit it and it will go off to the side . . . it's just not being right there . . . it's not being right there . . . it's not being right there . . . it's not being right . . .

T: *Yeah. I want you to swing that (bataca) . . . just swing that at the wall, but stop before you get to the wall.*

P: Out here?

T: Yeah, just feel what it's like to hold back . . . swing real hard but stop. [*Instructing him*] Feel that . . . stop . . . feel that . . . just feel that sensation.

P: [*Groaning*] That's what it's like . . . uh . . .

In this particular case and at this particular time, being afraid of getting hurt is not a feeling but an imaging coming from the patient's own disordering. It is by definition a secondary feeling. If he does follow through and subsequently gets hurt, *then* it would be a primary feeling. He needs to feel the consequences of holding back rather than the imaging, "I'll get hurt."

Actually, his defense and his feelings are closely related because holding back does hurt him. It is similar to the commonplace dream of trying to run away from something or someone and being unable to move fast enough. It is frustrating. All that is felt is the defense. There is no working through to the underlying feelings.

T: How does that [*Stopping*] feel to you?

P: It's tightening . . . you know, I can feel my throat tightening.

T: Right . . . your whole body tightens . . . no part of that swing is flowing . . . you are always ready to hold back . . . feel that in your whole body . . .

P: Yeah, I feel it up in here [*Pointing*] . . . I feel my . . .

T: Don't report it to me. Express that feeling.

It is now necessary to work with *how he expresses:* he is reporting rather than expressing. People often lose themselves by reporting with complete honesty every detail of what they did or did not do. It is often much more difficult to express from a feeling or a defense.[3]

Reporting is, in itself, a major defense and can only be overcome within an expressive therapy. Reporting is the same as picturing—it is the waking equivalent to passive dreaming. If reports are accurate they are similar to interpretations; if inaccurate they are similar to dream distortions. They represent a cognitive rather than an affective experiencing.

P: [*Loud groaning*] Ahh . . . that hurts my arm . . . aahh . . . aahh . . . I want to swing through.

T: No, really feel what it is like right now.

P: I feel it all in my arm, in my shoulder, right up to my neck . . . aahh . . . aagghh . . . Oh, that really feels bad . . . tightening up my whole shoulder . . . my arm aches so much . . . it just hurts.

T: That's right.

P: Really hurts . . . it hurts so much . . . I want to swing . . . I don't want to feel that . . .

T: Stay with the pain inside you . . . don't say what you want to do out there . . . Now I want you to swing . . . turn your whole body, get your whole body ready . . . and then stop it . . .

The therapist stops the patient from escaping or bypassing the defense. In fact, with these last instructions, the therapist further exaggerates the defense. The patient swings with all his might only to stop the swing before contacting the wall. He does not turn away from the feeling, but repeatedly experiences what holding back does to him.

It is important that the therapist continue to notice the *way* in which the patient expresses his feeling. He works to help the patient match his feeling (hurt) and his expression of it. He doesn't let him just say the words.

P: Oh, that hurts so much.

T: That's right . . . do that . . . your whole body . . . stop it.

P: Aahhh.

T: Don't say it hard . . . don't say it angry, because you're hurting. Say it like you are hurt.

P: [*Tightly*] I hurt.

T: No, let that sound out through that voice . . . no, loosen that voice up, really feel it.

P: I hurt.

T: Be tender with your body.

P: [*Sobbing*] I can't be . . . oh, my body hurts . . . oh, I can't be tender . . . [*Sobbing*] . . . Oh . . . [*Sobbing*]

T: That's it. Let it out.

P: [*Crying*] It hurts now to follow through . . . I can't follow through . . . I hurt.

At this point the therapy session is not a picture but an experience. This experiencing allows the patient to feel the effects of disordering on his waking life. He becomes aware of the way he operates from secondary feelings and pictures of feelings. He is finally *feeling his imaging*. The expression that results allows for the complete reversal of the disordering or imaging mechanisms.

STEP 3: THE ORGIN OF IMAGING

Now that it is isolated, the imaging can be *felt*. Instead of living unconsciously from images, the patient has expanded his personal image until it provokes a feeling great enough to be felt consciously.

His expression undoes the repression, and now he feels the source of the imaging ("I can't follow through") in his past, where he had experienced it, as a complete feeling (abreaction). But it is unrelated and contrary to the way he wants and needs to live his life now.

Just as ordinary dreams mix up fragments of past and present, this patient-dreamer mixes his day with present feelings and images derived from past disordering patterns. The therapist works to untangle the past and present, to separate the feeling and the imaging.

P: [*Crying*] I was thinking about these friends of mine who were in my dream last night. We were in the Jesuit order. They were all sitting at a table and they wouldn't even talk to me . . . all sitting there looking . . . I want them to talk.

T: Did you say that in your dream?

P: No, we were all sitting at these tables eating and my brother was sitting next to me . . . in my dream I was thinking . . .

T: That's holding back . . .

P: I was thinking, you know, "What's wrong? Why aren't they talking?"

T: When you were in the Jesuit order was it holding back for you?

P: It was holding back all the time . . . [*Crying*] I couldn't hold anybody . . . I could only talk during recreation, and then I could only talk to certain people during recreation . . . It feels bad . . . a boyhood friend of mine was with me in the Jesuit order. I couldn't even touch T. We grew up together. I had three four-year-old playmates. I couldn't even touch T.

It would be inaccurate to blame the patient's defenses on his past. He is responsible, ultimately, for his own behavior.

He made his own choice to join the Jesuit order, not seeing that he was unconsciously entering into a way of life that would sustain the old imaging pattern. In the next section we can see instead how painful it was for him to continue learning to hold back.

P: I tried talking to him but they really got him. You know, like I would talk about old times, then he would go and report it . . . got reported on for talking about old times when we weren't supposed to . . . [*Crying*] . . .

T: . . . you tried to follow through?

P: I wanted to . . . I tried a lot of times, you know, and then I'd end up just sort of fooling around and then get reported for it . . . I'd break the rules of modesty and I'd break the rules of silence . . . and I'd break the rules of touch.

T: But what were you trying to do?

P: I was trying to reach . . . [*Crying*]

T: Did you follow through with him?

P: No, I couldn't follow through with anybody. It was against the rules to follow through . . . Don't you understand, we had Rule 32.

T: No, what was Rule 32?

P: You shouldn't touch anybody . . . you shall not touch anybody . . . No one is to touch another except in a friendly gesture of hello or good-bye when they come or leave the house . . .

T: How does that feel to you? Not to follow through with your body?

P: That makes my hands get cold and numb . . . it feels bad.

In this exchange, we can hear that the patient is feeling the specific consequences of his defense ("my hands get cold and numb"). He is doing something in the therapy session that he had not been able to do earlier in his life—reach out. This is a small abreaction, but a critically important one.

The patient then talks and cries about his numb hands. The past and present become separated as he alternates between "giving my hands to God" and reaching out and touching his therapist.

P: [*Sobbing and holding hands as in prayer*] . . .

T: How does that feel?

P: That feels like nothing . . . I know that they are there, pressed against each other. I was thinking they would let me bless myself with my hands, and pray and give my hands to God . . . [*Reaching out*] . . . My hands are for touching . . . hands for blessing . . . Priests' hands are anointed . . . they annoint a priest's hands [*Crying*] . . . they are not for holding and caressing and loving [*Sobbing*] . . .

At this point he again felt what he had learned to do with his hands, how he had to whip himself, and write for hours a day until his arm was cramped. Over and over, he returned to the experience of reaching out and following through. He discovered how following through is letting his body relax and do what it really wants.

It is important to understand that even the simplest of movements, if done with full feeling, can be new and difficult. The patient reclaims parts of himself that were undeveloped in his past. He slowly learns to reach out, constantly supported and held in his feeling by his therapist.

T: Real slow.

P: [*Crying and sobbing*] . . .

T: There is so much more, now really go slow.

P: I can hardly stay there . . . I think . . .

T: I know, that's right. Don't think. Just really feel with your hands. What are they feeling?

P: [*Crying*] They are feeling soft skin and warm . . . so good . . . [*Sobbing*] . . .

T: Don't go away.

P: I do . . . I go away . . .

T: Just feel that . . . don't overload it . . . just use your fingertips now . . . just really explore . . . get your hands back.

He begins to feel that any discontinuity of feeling is "not following through." Any thought that stops his sensation and movement is holding back for him.

The therapist encourages this new movement to increase the patient's present feeling and helps him sustain the continuity of feeling that is necessary for integration. Being open does not mean being unafraid or defenseless; it means noticing every slight movement away from present reality and choosing to remain in feelingful self-contact. It is a process that will be enlarged and continued for a long period of time before this patient slowly transforms himself and reclaims his own body.

STEP 4: A NEW AFFECTIVE AWARENESS

There is a gentle shift toward bringing together the feeling of insights from the session. The patient does not try to conclude what is happening. He is integrated enough at this point to talk for himself without moving back. Insights are *about* feeling, but to be useful, they must emerge *from* feeling. Intellectual insights carry little momentum for change since the person has not felt the consequences of imaging, or the reward of feeling. Only affect insights have consequences.

> P: . . . That's right [*Crying*] that's really important . . . it's so important for me . . . because I make my . . . I really used to have such a bad time . . . when I don't follow through with K., the same thing happened to me night before last . . . I didn't sleep all night long . . . I should have told her . . .

> T: Just told her what?

> P: I didn't tell her enough . . . I didn't follow through by touching then, you know, and keep touching . . . I even tried "getting" through my words only . . .

> T: That's like being with Father C. in Seattle . . . how you didn't follow through then . . .

> P: Right . . . happy [*Crying*]. I'm sorta happy . . . I'm really happy, but I feel sad too . . . I was [*Sobbing*] . . .

> T: What?

> P: That's really important to me. I feel bad when I don't follow through. Yeah, especially I can feel that so much in here, my arm, my shoulder . . . when you had me holding that back.

We have stated as a matter of principle that dream function and waking function are parallel, and have used dreams and observations to support this contention. We have now shown this parallel using a psychotherapy session. There is little difference between the transformation psychotherapy session and the transformative dream. The functional processes we work with are identical.

This parallelism of function has very useful consequences.

It is a frequent limitation of most psychotherapies that the therapeutic intervention often seems external to the patient. He may want to change, but nevertheless feels the change is "forced on him." In his struggles, he unfortunately projects on the current relationship with his therapist past imaging patterns that frustrate and interfere with his own progress. Not eschewing countertransference, it would be nice to have a device available that diminishes this externalization, and makes it easier for the therapist and patient to deal with the patient's defenses and feelings.

Dreams are such a device. Our discovery of dream transformation assumes its greatest importance when we work with dreams in psychotherapy. The dream represents an internal reference point for the patient. It reduces as much as is possible the externalization of the therapy process.

In the next chapter we will show how we work with dreams. But it is important to remember that Functional Therapy is not just a dream therapy. We help the patient to learn to live out his or her own dream, in order to realize the potential for his or her own feeling. Incidents from any of the patient's activities—sex, play, work or fantasy—can be the focus of functional analysis.

9
WORKING WITH DREAMS IN THERAPY: AN EXAMPLE

A while back we showed, with the help of an excerpt from E.A. Abbott's *Flatland,* that a person evaluating human behavior must acquire a fresh vantage point in order to expand feelings and awareness. A new vantage point allows us to see more clearly where we are, and where we want to go. We need only to define the vantage point used to see where any psychological theory or practice is taking us.

Freud used associations to the normal dream for his perspective. He looked beyond the dreamer's overt content and tried to find hidden or latent contents. But for Freud, all that could ever naturally exist was the manifest content. Interpretation is external. Freud believed that it was impossible to understand dreams without outside intervention. We have made this point before, but we wish to add here that this view does not allow for any internal perspective. There is always a power outside the dreamer.

Jung correctly understood the prospective function of archetypal dreams but became lost in symbolic excursions because he never used the perspective that these dreams allow. Whether the dream movement is major, as in big dreams, or minor, as in little dreams, what matters is that movement toward expression occurs. Without this movement, big dreams such as the archetypal dream, become nothing more than bright jewels hidden away in a vault of partial consciousness, occasionally remembered but never used. Big dreams, such as archetypal dreams, present new images that lead toward more feeling in the dreamer's life. They do not need to be interpreted as Jung interpreted them. They need to lead the dreamer, or the potential within them will not be realized.

Unrealized potential is of no more value than no potential at all. A big dream calls for a functional completion of feeling in a person's dream life and waking life. For this reason, it is more important to focus on the transformative potential than the archetypal meanings.

The transformative dream is the vantage point in our functional approach. It provides an internal reference for an expanded potential of feeling. What is unique about this vision is that it is the dreamer's. It is not an imposed way of being (non-neurotic, undefended, normal) nor does it represent an imposed image (feelingful, sensible, dependable). It is a vision grounded in the dreamer's own experience of increased feeling and expression. He or she will follow that vision solely because of the joy of experiencing it.

The transformative dream represents a significant movement toward expression. At the most basic level there are only two directions of movement—toward feeling or away from feeling. At any point in any dream, the dreamer will be moving toward expression and matching, or away from expression and toward mismatching.

The transformative perspective suggests that a dreamer first allow himself to feel how he lives life at his present symbolic level of feeling. Secondly, the dreamer should feel what life could be like at an expanded level of feeling. Process questions lead to methods in which the dreamer is helped to return to the dream and feel how he functions in each dream picture. The dreamer is helped to become aware of the feelings left incomplete, and how this incompletion occurred. The specific further steps that result are not based on technique but rather on the dreamer and the particular dream.

There is little difference in the way we work with symbolic dreams or transformative dreams. In the latter, the work is already done — the dream has allowed the dreamer to feel his or her potential. All that remains is to live out the dream in order to sustain the feeling and expanded functional capabilities in waking life.

At any instant the way we express or defend ourselves is like a holographic unit or picture of the general way we express or deny our feelings. In an identical manner, the smallest part of the transformative dream is the symbolic dream. This dream or dream fragment is a microcosm of feeling and feeling potential enclosed and constrained by symbols.

When the two-dimensional normal dream fragment is expanded and projected utilizing the five dynamics, the entire picture of transformative feeling is vividly and multidimensionally present. Transformative movement within any dynamic heightens and broadens the entire feeling hologram.

Since the way we express or defend at each moment is part of our overall pattern of behavior, at any instant we have both our potential and our present limits in conflict with each other. It is the function of the therapist to bring this conflict into a conscious focus, and to aid the dreamer in reestablishing movement toward expression.

WORKING WITH THE DREAM[1]

FOCUSING THE CONFLICT

I don't remember a whole lot about it, but I woke up dreaming about J. (a therapist) who was wearing a bathing suit and we were standing in the street talking to some people and I'm not sure whether there

was a little boy there . . . a little five or six-year-old
boy . . . and I'm not sure whether I was that boy or
not. But the little boy was eating a piece of raw
chicken and . . . I don't remember too much about
the rest of it except that I think J. was saying it was
okay for him to do that . . . and my mother said I'd
get sick.

As the dreamer relates his dream he sounds vague and
disinterested — as though he were discussing a boring film he
had seen the night before. The way he dreams, relates his
dreams, and lives his life are identical. The session will be
directed toward the defenses he uses that keep him from being
an active part of his dream and waking life.

The therapist brings into focus the conflict between his
feeling potential, which is pictured in his dream by J., and his
present limits which are apparent both by the way he relates
the dream and in the picture of his mother. He will be forced
to feel each picture.

P: In the dream, J. seemed really nice and I remember in the dream that I was thinking that the
chicken might not be good for him, but J. really
knew. J. was like saying, "No, it's okay."

T: Did the boy like the raw chicken?

P: Yeah. [*More excited, more awake*] He was really
just eating it. Yeah.

The dreamer (M.) became more expressive as he talked
about eating the raw chicken. The therapist noted that M.
enjoyed the affect associated with the boy. He became enthus-
iastic, finally admitting to liking the chicken, a feeling he omit-
ted when originally reporting the dream. In his initial dream
report he seemed disconnected and confused. In waking, he
often acts confused when he is not. Instead of responding to

the impulse of the moment, he separates himself from his feelings and those around him.

On further questioning by the therapist, M. stopped his enthusiasm and expressiveness by talking about the likelihood of getting sick from eating raw chicken. Both in the dream, and while relating the dream, he stops himself from complete expression. In his dream he projects his defense on his mother who sounds very reasonable. During the day, he himself sounds very reasonable.

For a patient who is reasonable, the session must provide more than just another reason for certain behavior. His own feeling must permit him to choose when and how much to express. He doesn't need reasons or interpretations; he needs to feel and express himself.

T: If the boy could talk, what would he say back to you in the dream?

P: [*Answers with a shrug of his shoulders*] Probably he'd say, "I want the chicken."

T: Would he just shrug it off like that?

P: No.

T: Well, how would he say it?

P: "I want the chicken, I want it. That's all, I want it."

The therapist noted that M. was not feeling what he was saying. He was mouthing empty words. She responded immediately.

T: I don't believe you.

P: That's the way I think a little child would say it.

T: Would he hesitate after each word and look up and check it out?

P: What *I* think of doing is taking it and running.

T: Do you run away?

P: Yeah. I do that a lot.

T: Talk.

P: I do that a lot with people. Instead of sticking and talking to people, I'll just stop and skip over things.

T: Right now, M. You're doing it right now. You're giving me a very concrete explanation. You're hiding behind those words.

At this time the therapist was aware that M. was going through the motions of talking to her, that he was being "reasonable" as he generalized about himself. She countered by not allowing him to break contact, forcing him to look and talk right to her.

T: Look at me.

P: When I started talking about running away I started getting sad.

T: Do you want to hide?

P: No, I don't. I just do that. You know, the way I'd take it and run and be safe with it so that nobody can take it away from me. [*Crying*] So that nobody can pick on me . . . be alone somewhere, alone in a closet or somewhere away from that person. *There's no point in staying around and saying anything and doing anything. Just take it and run.* [*Crying throughout*] . . .

The conflict between expressing and stopping is coming into focus. It is really a conflict of past and present. "There is no point in staying around and saying anything and doing anything," is a statement from his past that affects his present level of role and expression. Contrast this with the following.

168   DREAMS IN THERAPY

P: . . . And then it's not like that little kid in the dream. That little kid in the dream. Standing there and just loving it and . . . [*Crying*] . . . *J. would say . . . It's okay, it's okay.* It's not nice — that kid was having the chicken plus he was having J. say it's okay to these other people.

"J. would say it's okay," is a statement from his present life that confirms and strengthens his own feeling, role and clarity: It is "okay" to want and act from feeling.

EXPANDING THE CONFLICT

The conflict represented in the dream creates a mix that prevents him from being naturally aggressive. The mixing shows up equally in his dream (mother is *past,* J. is *present*) and in waking (reasonableness is *past,* expressiveness is *present*). In order to unmix past from present, the dreamer has to take on all the feelings in the dream as his own.

At this time he projects his defense on his mother and his fight to respond fully on J. He needs to take responsibility for his own defenses and his own expression. Otherwise he will continue to live from projections of his feelings on others, rather than living from within himself.

T: What did the boy think when he heard J. say that?

P: [*Crying*] "That's okay, it's okay. He knows what's right. He's letting me do it."

T: Do what?

P: What you want. It's okay. He was eating out in the street. There were other people around and that's something my mother told me never to do. [*Crying*] Like at the end of a meal, someone would take a piece of cake or watermelon or something and go out in the street. She'd say, "No, don't do that. You shouldn't do that in the street. You shouldn't let other people see you eating." And in this dream J. was standing there saying that it was okay that the kid was in the street eating, and it was okay that it wasn't cooked, and the kid wasn't dressed up. He was wearing a pair of shorts and shoes and no shirt or anything. That was okay. [*Crying*]

T: Would that be okay with your mother?

P: No. No.

T: How come?

P: Because of appearances.

T: What did she want? How did she want you to dress?

P: Neat and clean and respectable and be a good boy. Shine my shoes, clean socks, and pants and a shirt. Got to wear a shirt, too.

T: What would J. say to her?

P: Leave him alone!

T: Say that.

P: Leave him alone. Stop badgering him. Stop badgering him. Stop picking on him . . . picking on him and poking at him. [*Crying*]

T: Go on.

P: Stop picking on him and poking at him . . . he's just a kid, leave him alone. It's okay. It's okay. [*Crying*] It's okay. There's nothing wrong with what he's doing.

T: Tell her that.

P: There's nothing wrong with what I'm doing.
There's nothing wrong with it. [*Crying*] There's
nothing wrong with it at all. There's nothing
wrong with it. [*Crying*]

It is a common misconception in abreactive psychotherapies that going back to the emotions of the past means *leaving*
the present. In reality there is no past—there is only the way
the past has shaped present behavior. When a patient such as
M. experiences feeling from the past, he is really experiencing
the pain of using old defenses from the past in the present.
He will not change if he limits himself to the expression of past
feeling. He must lift his defenses if he is to make contact with
the therapist. The past, just like a dream, has no real meaning
unless it helps to strengthen contact in the present.

In this case, just as he begins to feel and express the words
that he had to conceal as a child, he stops. After a brief pause
the therapist asked:

T: What'd you just think?

P: All those reasonable things I heard her saying.
"You could get sick. You could get sick." What
J. was saying was real nice, but suppose he could
get sick. Suppose he could get sick.

T: Who's that talking?

P: That's my mother or me, I'm not sure. Maybe
both.

T: Uh-huh. Now, what would J. say to your mother?

P: Shut up and leave him alone. Getting sick doesn't
matter. It doesn't matter!

T: Say it again.

P: It doesn't matter at all. In the dream that little
kid . . . every little bite, every bite was so deli-

cious, he was just biting on it and eating it and it was so delicious it didn't matter. It didn't matter, didn't matter . . . it doesn't matter at all.

T: Now, really say that.

P: It really doesn't matter. [*Crying*]

The therapist noted: "I know the hardest thing for him to do is to *be* as powerful as he is. I feel him backing down the tiniest bit by crying. It's important (since he can cry so easily) that he maintain those feelings inside his body (not try to get rid of them in the shape of tears) and use them as a force and power behind his words."

T: Say it without crying.

P: It doesn't matter at all. It doesn't matter at all. It doesn't matter at all. It doesn't . . . it just doesn't matter. [*Crying*] It doesn't make any difference to what's going on. I want the chicken.

T: Say that.

P: I want the chicken. I like it, and I like eating it, and I love eating it in the street, and I don't care about getting sick. *I'm not sick now. I'm not throwing up now.*

The therapist stops him immediately. "I'm not sick now" is a *reason* to continue eating the chicken or continue the expression. In effect, he still believes that "it does matter." Instead of being a good boy, he is a good patient. There is not much difference. He is "the reasonable patient" doing what he *should* do, but he has lost how he feels.

One of the flaws of technique-oriented therapies is the ability of patients to perform a given technique. If this therapist did not have feeling contact with herself and the patient, she might have accepted the patient's performance as long as it matched theoretical background. A technique should be

created at the right moment, and discarded as soon as contact has been made. What is important is the contact between
two people, and not the technique.

T: Was that boy reasonable? Did he use his reason
    when he picked up the chicken?

P: No. He didn't think about anything except want-
    ing that chicken.

T: Does that boy want to be reasonable when he's
    trying to tell his mom something?

P: [*Crying*] I think that's why I'm saying to the kid,
    "Run, run." You know, because he's going to
    lose. [*Crying*]

T: Tell him that.

P: You've got to run and get away from her. [*Cry-
    ing*] Because you can't win, *you can't just . . .
    just say "I want it" and have it be enough.* You
    can't do that. You know you're going to take it
    and run. Take it and run and get away. [*Crying*]
    Just take it and run.

This is a perfect summation of his childhood. He had to
do more than just live — he had to be convincing, reasonable
and believable. What follows is a turning point in the session.
He is ready to break the pattern of his past and begin to assume
the power J. had in his dream.

REMOVING THE CONFLICT

P: [*Crying*] . . . I feel like what I'm ready to do is
    stay and protect him.

T: Tell him.

P: [*Crying*] . . . I'll stay and protect you. You
    know, I'd like to stay and stand up for you.

T: How would you protect him?

P: By making her go away.

T: How?

P: [*Crying*] By yelling at her, or pushing her or just grabbing her and pushing her away.

T: How would you push her away?

P: With my hands. I'd push her like that.

T: Do that.

P: Just like that.

As the patient expresses, he begins to move his arms in an outward and forceful manner. He seems to punctuate each sentence with his upper body. This new movement, taken from the dream, can be used to maintain the expanded role after the session is completed.

The therapist notes that this movement helps to increase the feeling level deeper in the patient's body. He was full of anger that had been locked behind "reasons" for many years. His voice no longer seemed lodged in a constricted throat. Further, he had his *own movement* now instead of the symbolic movement of running away. He had a movement that matched his expression.

He would return to his defense and would stop expression for a number of reasons throughout the rest of the session. These reasons included a headache, getting tired, and suffering a bruised hand. In each instance he was allowed to return to full expression and his new movement. The reason quickly vanished.

By the end of the session he was able to talk about the dream in a way that was qualitatively different:

P: You know, I don't have to respond as though I'm living with my mother.

T: Do you have to run away, M., to be this strong and to be . . .

P: No. That's how I get weak. I make my own grounds, set my own terms.

T: Do you need J.?

P: No, no, I don't.

T: That was you, too, in that dream. That's this part of you.

P: That's true. But that was me coming out with the chicken into the street.

T: Snap your arms forward.

P: That was me coming out by myself. [*Gesturing*] I'm not asking permission. J. didn't give me the permission in the dream and say it's okay to come out with the chicken. I did that because I wanted to. [*Yelling*] Just walked out the way I was. And I was standing there eating it before anybody said it was okay. I was standing there eating it. Munching it. I would feel it dribbling down my face. And that's me. That's me.

T: Say it strong. Snap it!

P: That's me! That's me *inside!* I am so alive. I don't want to run away and hide! I don't want to explain anything! I don't have to stop!

The patient begins defended and ends connected to the way he can be. However, this session does not represent anything more than a beginning. The patient must use his new movement and awareness each time he finds himself less expressive than he knows he is. He has to choose to move along a path that seems strange yet wonderfully promising. The only difference between his journey before and after this therapy session is that he now has an internal awareness of his own destination. He has seen himself from a new perspective provided by the expansion of his own dream.

A patient can choose to be defensive, or expressive. It is the way he or she responds to life following a psychotherapeutic session that will create change and lead to transformation. If functional analysis doesn't move the person to new modes of behaving outside the therapy session, it becomes just another way of interpreting dreams.

We can use dreams to follow the therapeutic movement during waking. In the case we have just cited, as the patient began to change his life, his dreaming changed as well. A week later he reported the following dream:

> *I was trying to fly. I kept jumping up and down waving my arms. It didn't work. I tried three or four times but would barely get off the ground. I was afraid I'd fall. Then I didn't care if I would fall and just leaned forward. I sort of glided over the ground, just a few feet in the air. My arms were outstretched. It was my way to fly. I never saw anyone fly that way before. I loved the sensation.*

The feeling of flying was one of power, and of powerful sensations in his body. It was distinctly his way of flying that meant so much to him. His way of expressing was not acquired in his past, or from a present outside source. What was significant was not that he had a power dream, but that he was changing his life. This dream was both an index of his progress and another reference in his movement from here to there. The transformative dream provides a standard of positive functioning[2] that is both a personal experience and a reportable event. It can be described, reproduced and measured.

10
DREAMS AND HUMAN WELFARE

Sleep! Sleep!
In the land of dreams
Find your grown-up self
Your future family
Sleep! Sleep!
> (Wintu Song, Kroeber and Heizer, 1967,
> *Almost Ancestors,* p. 65)

What influences could dream transformation have on human welfare? The contemporary Western world is a peculiarly impoverished community. We have been cognitively creative but not affectively creative in manufacturing our technology. Technology has made it seem unnecessary to sense external events keenly; it is used as a buffer in the environment. As a result, expressing feeling no longer appears to be an evolutionarily significant talent. Unfortunately, it often seems unnecessary to sense and express internal events as well. But it is these internal events that connect people to one another.

Technology comes between people. A media technology develops to remove the immediacy of moment-to-moment contact. We have technological knowledge of the outer world, but very little knowledge of the inner world, and consequently very little communicating. Communicating and community depend upon person-to-person exchanges. Today, most children grow up in a media-dominant culture, not a contact culture.

MEDIA CULTURE VS. CONTACT CULTURE

A media culture is characterized by ways of communication where the listener's or viewer's responses do not immediately affect the messages of the sender. In a contact culture the exchanges between two or more people affect each other. The medium of exchange can be gestures, touches, speech, or all three, but every contact culture encourages simultaneous responsive communication in which the outcome is the natural result of the participants' feelings. Only in a contact culture can feelings be shown; a media culture can evoke feelings but there is no way to share and change them.

The basic human culture is contact culture. The brain's abilities to exchange signs and symbols and to sense and respond to feelings are interconnected.[1] Although there is no necessary conflict between media cultures and contact cultures, just as there is no necessary intracortical conflict, our own culture has become media-dominant.

There are two serious consequences of the dominance of media messages over contact exchanges. First, contact culture becomes shrunken and distorted and the forms of contact become pathological. Second, media images and symbols of how to be and what to do replace feelings of being and doing. Affective functioning depends upon responsive, flexible exchanges and cannot be taught through the media—all that can be taught are ways to act and appear. As contact exchanges are replaced by media imitations, the brain's ability to exchange signs and signals begins to dominate its ability to sense and respond to feelings.

Because of the loss of feeling function, a person reared in a media culture finds making the private public both frightening and strange. The media person will mistake the communication of facts about someone for expressions of feeling from someone. Such a person will believe he knows someone when he merely knows about him or her and will not really recognize the experience of hearing from another person. The media person does not want his privacy invaded; his thoughts and feelings are his private property.

This desire for privacy is one of the biggest barriers to transformative dreaming. Until it is overcome, dreams remain private and symbolic and distinct from public reality. Media-dependent people do not have the inner reality or the outer community to support transformative dreaming. Dream transformation cannot be taught in a book or film or on television.[2] It must come about person-to-person.

The great social value of a shared functional approach to dreams is that:

1. It enhances the individual dreamer's awareness of how he or she lives.
2. It enhances other people's awareness of the dreamer.
3. It develops a mutual awareness of the functional processes that make for good or bad feeling inside a person and between people.

In short, it is a method of developing inner experiences and interpersonal happenings.

RECOVERING WHAT WE HAVE LOST

We do not advocate a return to preliterate cultural forms. Instead we want to point the way to new cultural forms. There is no advantage in returning to preliterate ways of life because such cultures which are ruled by fixed rituals are as media-dominant as the most advanced technological cultures. There is no essential difference between a native New Guinean who projects his or her feelings onto outside spirits and controls them by observing taboos, and a native American who projects his or her feelings on media stars and controls those feelings by taking tranquilizers and mood elevators.

Jung reports a story about his contacts with the Pueblo Indians:

> They told me that all Americans are crazy, and of course I was somewhat astonished and asked them why. They said, "Well, they say they think in their heads. No sound man thinks in the head. *We* think in the heart." . . . our concept of consciousness supposes thought to be in our most dignified head. But the Pueblo Indians derive consciousness from the intensity of feeling. (Jung, *Memories, Dreams, Reflections,* 1961, p. 9)

Certain American Indians understood something that our media-dominant culture does not: connectedness. All life connects to other life and to nonlife. The basis of connectedness is feeling. A media-dominant culture loses its connectedness. And media dominant people become consumers and advertisers rather than dream makers. The Indians talked about "loss of soul;" we talk about insanity and "loss of feeling"—they are the same.

Contemporary psychotherapists are like the old teachers and shamans and tribal leaders—they try to help people reclaim what they have lost. Because they have no tribe or tradition to sustain them, the therapists have less inner and outer power. But it is possible to reclaim our lost heritage. The human condition is to be found not only in the outward aspirations of technological civilization and research but in the inward return to community and inner life. The dream can be a good guide to the inner life because no matter how disordered outer reality becomes, there is still an inward, dominant impulse to feeling completion with each nightly passage into dreaming. Not even the most disconnected person can do without sleep and dreams. Many American Indian groups understood this connecting function of dreaming and organized their lives around dream exchanges as the basis of contact culture.

> The direct (Yuman) basis of all religion, tradition, ritual song, and a shamanistic power is individual dreaming . . . The dreamer went sometimes on a fabulous dream-journey, but more often he succeeded in summoning to himself the spirit of a Hero, a Creator-God, or an authoritarian Bird or Animal or Fish who spoke to him as it had spoken in the days before men were put on earth. The Spirit could be expected, having come, to make the dreamer-petitioner a personal gift of knowledge or skill or power with instructions for its use and increase. (Kroeber and Heizer, 1967, p. 45, 129)

It is a remarkable and pleasing paradox that dreaming, the seemingly most useless and impractical of human activities, can be the foundation for the education of vital affective capabilities. We believe that the abilities to dream transformative dreams and function at the highest levels of expression, clarity, activity and feeling are as important as the abilities to read, write and do arithmetic. Fortunately, affective education is no harder than cognitive education.

People can be dream makers again. People can choose between making dreams or being taken over by disordered images. The same choice is present in waking life. People can make their lives, or be taken over by images that are advertisements of life. They can choose to become creative in a new way. It is this choice that we are writing about when we talk of transformation.

The shift away from media dominance to a balance between the head and heart is also a shift with evolutionary significance. The human organism evolved to function from complete feelings; any cultural milieu that does not support such functioning hurts the organism. A contact culture can support complete feelings, a media-dominant culture cannot.

In his book, *The Expression of Emotions in Man and Animals,* Darwin states emphatically that the ways of expressing emotion are adaptively necessary. It is unfortunate that Darwin's emphasis on the survival value of expressiveness has not been taken seriously by many contemporary biologists and psychologists. His arguments were ignored because they do not fit easily into a behavioristic theory. Darwin was not talking about emotional behavior; he was concerned with emotional expressiveness. If this crucial difference is slighted, then research becomes misdirected and unproductive.[3]

Darwin could make the following observation because he was not confined within the behavioristic limitations.

> Baboons seem to act consciously when they threaten by opening their mouths and showing their great canine teeth; for Mr. Bartlett has had species with their canine teeth sawn off, and these never acted in this manner. *They would not show their comrades they were powerless* [our emphasis]. (Darwin from Ekman, *Darwin and Facial Expression,* 1973, p. 261)

A behaviorist or objectivist would label such interpretations anthropomorphic. But unless we consider consciousness and expressiveness instead of stimuli and responses, these observations about baboons are not correctly interpreted.[4]

The last half-century in psychology has been dominated by two conflicting orientations: behaviorism and psychoanalysis. The psychoanalytic emphasis is on insight, seeking an understanding of why something is done or not done. The behavioristic emphasis is on prediction and control, attempting a change in *what* is done or not done. Of course, there are many crossovers. Psychoanalysts want their patients to change and behavior therapists aim for basic alterations which include more than one form of behavior.

Perry London, in *Modes and Morals of Psychotherapy,* characterizes these two broad orientations as "Insight Therapies" and "Action Therapies":

> If the therapist is oriented toward insight methods, he will probably try to assail the ailment that lies beneath the symptom, bypassing the immediate problem. If he is an Action Therapist, he will probably behave as if the symptom were itself ailment enough, and try to remove it. From another angle, the Insight Therapist will try to help his patient with the reflected problem rather than the symptom, thus undermining the symptom or at least permitting the patient to understand the character of his symptom and its relationship to his life so that he can exercise better control over the latter if not the former. The Action Therapist will try more directly to eliminate the symptom so that the patient will feel better, and it makes no difference to him what the patient does or does not understand about anything. (London, 1964, pp. 34-36)

When working with dreams, the Insight Therapist helps the patient to understand what a dream means; the Action Therapist usually doesn't work with dreams at all though the therapist will try to help a person alter the nighttime anxiety attacks called nightmares. One approach emphasizes understanding and interpretation, the other, control. Neither takes a transformative approach to dreaming because neither is a transformative approach to living.

Functional therapies such as Gestalt Therapy, Client-Centered Therapy, and Functional Psychotherapy share these emphases:

1. Feelings are used as conscious mediators of personality change.

2. The therapies focus on expression rather than behavior or insight.

3. They stress dynamics of expressiveness rather than expressive content.

4. They are concerned with optimal functioning rather than just normal or adaptive functioning.

5. They examine the need for community in therapeutic change.

They differ from both the Analytic-Experiential Therapies and the Behavior-Modification Therapies by concerning themselves with both inner experiencing and outer expression. The Functional Therapies bridge the action and insight sides of human life through expression. A person is fully expressive only when that individual's outer behavior matches his or her inner experience. It is possible to condition reactions without this matching. And it is possible to insightfully understand without matching. But it is not possible to be fully expressive unless something inside is being fully shown outside.

This simple emphasis on expression has far-reaching implications. By focusing on expression rather than empty actions or reactions or behaviors, we emphasize the necessary connection between behavior and experience. It is the absence of this connection, or the mismatching of behavior and experience, which constitutes psychopathology. It is our belief that expression and expressiveness are the major components of psychotherapy, and more basically, of daily life.

Although dreams are internal, private, and personal, the transformation of dreams cannot be furthered unless they are also recognized as attempts to complete expression. From this functional orientation, the dream then can be made external, public and socially significant. It becomes an immediate form of exchange. The functional approach synthesizes personal and social levels. On the personal level the bridge between the

Insight-Experientialists and the Behaviorists is accomplished through expression. By sharing what is inside, a person is forced to live out his or her own theories and personal approaches, exposing them and feeling them more intensely because they are expressed. Individuals are modified and encouraged by those around them.

Synthesis on a broader social level is accomplished by a community. A community provides the time and the place—a time to expand on the movement of the therapy and a place within which to move. Since to become functional, a theory or therapy must be pushed to its limits and beyond, people must live out their insights and associations. They must live out their responses to others. The therapeutic process must follow the person as he or she functions throughout the entire day. Only then will the theorist and therapist find out what the ultimate weaknesses and omissions are in their approach. Only then will they be able to change the way they live to make their lives and theories complete.

The term "transformation" can mean either "a change in the form or outward appearance" or "a change in the condition and nature" (*Webster's New World Dictionary*, 1957, pp. 1546-47). What we have said about the transformation of dreams and the functional orientation to dreaming emphasizes both meanings. *Expressing a felt reality lets people be in the world and change the world. Inner transformation and outer transformation are the same—in waking and dreaming.*

We began this book by relating a dream. We called that dream a transformative dream and showed that, in such dreams, the dreamer functions differently than in normal dreams. We then went on to show that normal symbolic dreams exhibit mainly distinctions of reality and malfunctioning, while transformative dreams reveal reality and full functioning.

If symbolic dreams are taken as the standard of human

emotionality then it is not odd that analyzing would come to mean understanding and controlling emotions. But if transformative dreams are taken as a new standard then analyzing must mean both understanding and expressing. We used transformative dreaming as a model for what psychotherapy sessions could be and dreamer communities as models for therapeutic communities.

In this final chapter, we will close by suggesting that transformative dreaming can be a model for civilization. In humanity's search for a better way of life, the intellect and individual achievements have often been glorified at the expense of feelings and group achievements. This imbalance does not make use of the human being's full evolutionary potential. We believe affective capabilities can be developed to be as subtle and sophisticated as cognitive capabilities. When this balance is achieved in human development we will shift from a symbolic civilization to a transformative civilization.

HOW TO USE DREAMS FOR PSYCHOLOGICAL FITNESS TRAINING

One way to understand dreams is to look at dreaming as a form of emotional exercise that each of us does every night. This understanding is in line with the functional emphasis on *how* we dream rather than *what* we dream.[5] It is more important to know how fast and how far someone jogs and how long he or she sustains an increased pulse rate and how long it takes for the pulse to return to normal than it is to know where the person ran or what the runner saw while jogging. In the same way it is more important to know how effectively people function in their dreams than what they dream about.

Dreams can be used as both an indicator of how psychologically fit a person is and as a vehicle for psychological fitness training.

To quickly assess how effectively your sleep and dreams are functioning take this Sleep and Dream Checkup.

SLEEP AND DREAM FITNESS

	YES	NO
1. Do you use your dreams to help yourself understand and change your life?	____	____
2. Do you have the skills you need to understand and use your dreams?	____	____
3. Are you satisfied with your dream life?	____	____
4. Generally, do you feel good in your dreams?	____	____
5. Do you remember your dreams three times a week?	____	____
6. Do you discuss your dreams with friends and acquaintances at least once a week?	____	____
7. Do you feel rested and alert upon waking?	____	____
8. Do you sleep soundly?	____	____
9. Do you fall asleep easily and naturally without drugs or alcohol?	____	____
10. Are you satisfied with your sleep fitness?	____	____
TOTAL	____	____

8–10 yeses. You are dreaming effectively. You can begin making a few exercise adjustments, and you will have a consistent peak performance from your sleep and dreams. Your score suggests that your inner self and your outer self are getting closer together. The more you allow yourself to take action in waking experience, the more you experience the cycle of psychological fitness (from waking to dreams to waking). Here are some exercises you can do to begin exercising your dream personality.

1. Start taking a look at your dream personality. How active, how expressive, how feelingful, how clear are you and how much contact do you make in your dreams? If you are low in any of these categories you need some more work. Notice that how you are in your dreams is often how you are in waking.

2. Take your dreams seriously. Remember you are the dream maker. Listen to what you are telling yourself about yourself.

3. Start your own dream group. Once a week meet with your family or friends and exchange dreams.

   4–7 yeses. You are an average dreamer. This means that your inner self and your outer self are far enough apart that the only way they make contact with each other is through symbols in your dreams. You need to begin facing the symbolic nature of the communication between your inner and outer self. At night your inner self is taking over and telling you how well your personality is really functioning. Here are some dream *Do's and Don'ts.*

DON'T

1. Don't try to interpret your dreams. Don't look for sexual or psychological meaning behind every symbol.

2. Don't try to control your dreams by programming them before you go to bed at night.

3. Don't keep a written dream diary, yet. Later you can record your most important dreams, once you know how to use them.

4. Don't use the dream books which tell you forty thousand dreams and their meaning.

DO

1. In the morning when you wake up and want to remember your dreams, ask yourself, "How do I feel?" Dreams are pictures of feelings, and you need to get in touch with the feelings first; the pictures will come naturally when you remember the feeling.

2. If you can't remember a dream, make one up based on the feeling you awakened with. Just make up a simple dream, with pictures and dialogue.

3. Do talk every day with one other person about your dream, and about how you felt while asleep.

4. Do make sure that you have a good and consistent sleep schedule. Make sure your body gets the rest it needs. Research has shown that we need seven to eight hours per night on the average. However, everyone has his or her own patterns and specific needs. Become aware of what sleep schedule feels best to you and stick to it.

1–3 yeses. You are a dream spectator. A large part of your life is beyond your reach. Your inner self and outer self are doing battle during the night. It's time you brought some light and understanding into your sleep and dream life. Remembering your dreams is a first step. Set your clock for one half hour earlier than you normally wake up. As soon as you get up, be aware of how you feel. Start writing down whatever you are feeling and thinking, even sentence fragments. Your low score indicates that your waking personality is not functioning up to its potential. You need to concentrate more on it while looking to your sleep and dreams to verify the results of what you are doing.

Think of five important activities that you regularly perform. Every day, in your dream diary, complete the following phrases in reference to those activities.

1. I would like to be more active when . . .

2. I would like to be more expressive when . . .

3. I would like to feel more when . . .

4. I would like to have more clarity when . . .

5. I would like to make more contact when . . .

These are *remembering exercises*. The more that you do them, the more you will remember that you have an inner self. When you remember your inner self, you will begin remembering your dreams and will become aware of how your dream personality is functioning. Once you remember your dreams, answering these simple questions will help you work with your dreams.

1. If I were more active in this dream, then . . .

2. If I were more expressive in this dream, then . . .

3. If I felt more in this dream, then . . .

4. If I were clearer in this dream, then . . .

5. If I made more contact in this dream, then . . .

If you ask yourself these questions for each dream you remember, you will begin exercising your dream personality. It will get stronger and your next checkup score should improve dramatically.

APPENDIX

THE PROCESS SCALES FOR FUNCTIONALLY ANALYZING DREAMS

A functional analyst of dreams looks at how effectively the dreamer's personality is functioning. Functional analyses disregard the what and why of the dream, at least initially, and look instead at how the dreamer functions in his or her own dream. The basic functional question is: How effectively does the dreamer function in this dream?

The five basic personality characteristics that are examined are:

1. **Feeling level:** refers to the individual's overall feeling level or emotional tone.

2. **Role level:** refers to the specific physical actions an individual takes in response to various events and emotional interactions.

3. **Clarity level:** measures the level of awareness the individual has of his or her internal state in relation to external events.

4. **Expression level:** measures how intensely the individual shows feelings about events and interactions.

5. **Contact level:** defines the degree to which an individual affects and allows him- or herself to be affected by others.

The first scale, **Feeling,** is used in a broad sense. The category definitions are:

(5) Intense: The feeling dominates the dream; feeling overrides all else in dream, e.g., prolonged crying, screaming, anger, terror, dreams of danger, life threatening situations, intense reliving of childhood feelings, ecstasy.

(4) Strong: Definite feeling, more than what is usually evident in normal waking life, but feeling does not dominate entire dream.

(3) Moderate: There is some feeling. The feeling is not vague and in the background but does not dominate or even greatly influence the dream picture.

(2) Slight: The dream itself evokes some feeling response in the scorer. The feeling, however, is vague and in the background.

(1) No feeling: Dreams about things or events that remain affectively neutral. The dream has no effect on scorer; there is no obvious content which might evoke feeling.

The second scale, **Role,** is about the actions of the dreamer. It measures the quality of the dreamer's actions (not the quantity of general activity). The scale definitions are:

(5) Fully active: Dreamer's role in response to dream events is complete. His activity is dominating, striking, totally responsive, initiates action, frequently changes consequences of dream.

(4) Active: Dreamer's role in response to dream events is full but there is more he or she could be doing in response to dream event. Actively involved in course of dream, may change consequences.

(3) Slightly active: There is some response by dreamer to dream events. But for the most part dreamer's role does not alter the dream outcome.

(2) Passive: The dreamer is only a part of the dream. His or her role is that of being present, uninvolved or unresponsive.

(1) No Role: The dreamer has no role in the dream.

The third scale, **Clarity,** is about how easily understandable the dream is. It is concerned with the what and why within the dream. The scale definitions are:

(5) Completely clear and direct: The feelings in the dream are clear and evident to the scorer. The actions of the dream are coherent in themselves. The dream picture makes sense. No distortion.

(4) Clear and direct: For the most part the dream feelings and actions make sense in themselves. The picture is clear and direct but not complete. Minor distortions.

(3) Somewhat clear and direct: The scorer has a general idea of what is going on in the dream feelings and actions. But there is an incomplete development of dream picture. Some elements may be distorted.

(2) Unclear and indirect: There is much distortion but it does not completely obscure the dream picture. The dream picture is unclear. There is incomplete development of dream picture. Feelings and events are disconnected. Very little idea of what is happening, no idea why.

(1) Completely confused: The dream picture is incoherent. Distortion dominates. Events and feelings have no relationship. Many elements are hazy and undefined. No development of dream theme.

The fourth scale, **Expression,** is about how intensely the dreamer shows his or her feelings about the dream events or interactions. It measures the quality of the dreamer's expression. The scale definitions are:

(5) Intense: Prolonged and complete expression of feelings.

Expression completely dominates the dream. The dreamer continues to express even in the face of obstacles. Total expression. Striking and definite. Dreamer is not confined in any expressions by any of the events or characters.

(4) Strong: Expression that takes preference over all other dreamer activities but is not prolonged or does not dominate the entire dream.

(3) Moderate: Definite but not striking expression. Clearly does not dominate the dreamer's activity and is only part of the overall dream picture.

(2) Slight: Some expression but relegated to a minor feature of the dream. The dreamer's expression is not a striking feature of the dream.

(1) No expression: No observable expression of any feelings or thoughts by the dreamer. There is no manifest display of internal dreamer situation.

The fifth scale, **Contact,** refers to how much contact with other people the dreamer makes in the dream. The scale points are:

(5) Full contact: The dreamer moves toward friends and others in the dream. There is no avoidance of emotional contacts. The dreamer actually touches other people in the dream.

(4) Strong contact: Movement toward others is strong but not always complete.

(3) Moderate contact: There is more movement toward than away.

(2) Slight contact: There is more movement away than toward. Strangers predominate.

(1) No contact: No other people in dream or all movement is away from physical contact with others.

NOTES

Complete references can be found in the Bibliography.

CHAPTER 1

1. This experience of chaos and the therapy that emerged from it are described by Hart, Corriere and Binder, *Going Sane: An Introduction to Feeling Therapy.* New York: Dell Publishing Co., 1976. A shorter introduction to this therapy can be found in Karle, Woldenberg, & Hart, "Feeling Therapy: Transformation in Psychotherapy" in Binder, Binder and Rimland (Eds.), *Modern Therapies.* New York: Prentice Hall, 1976.

2. A popular account of our personal experiences is reported in Corriere and Hart, *The Dream Makers: Discovering Your Breakthrough Dreams,* Part II. New York: Funk and Wagnalls, 1977; Bantam, 1978.

3. Feeling Therapy is also sometimes referred to as Functional Therapy or Functional Psychotherapy. Both labels are correct. See "Questions and Answers about Feeling Therapy" and the "Functional School of Psychotherapy." *Center Newsletter,* 1977, Vol. I, No. 6, available from The Center Foundation.

4. Consult *The Dream Makers,* Part III, for a complete guided program of exercises in applying the functional approach to individual dreams. There are also sections on the practical use of dreams in Corriere and Hart, *Psychological Fitness.* New York: Harcourt Brace Jovanovich, 1979.

CHAPTER 2

1. The Cognitive Drive is also termed motivation competence by White, *Psychological Review*, 1959, *66*, 297–333, and the manipulation drive by Harlow, *Journal of Experimental Psychology*, 1950, *40*, 228–34.

2. A modern theory of feeling with which we have much in agreement is that of Dr. Manfred Clynes, *Sentics: The Touch of Emotions*, New York: Doubleday, 1977. Dr. Clynes' theory is based largely upon psychophysiology and experimental aesthetics while ours is drawn largely from clinical observations but they are in substantial agreement that experiencing and expression should not be separated.

CHAPTER 3

1. An expansion and clarification of these ideas will be presented in Chapter 9. In *The Dream Makers* we describe how the functional approach can be used outside a therapeutic setting for affective education.

2. See Chapter 6.

3. For more about these five interpersonal dynamics, see the *Appendix*.

4. Dream interpretation (understanding a dream) and dream transformation (expressing feelings in a dream) can be complementary. Transformation supercedes interpretation. It is not possible to transform a dream without also understanding it, but it is possible to understand a dream without feeling it or changing from the symbolic feeling representation to nonsymbolic feeling expressions. This is a basic limitation of any analytic theory and therapy. If a patient becomes so overfocused on understanding his or her dream life and waking life that he or she does not feel and change the way he or she lives, then interpretation has become a defensive activity. See Chapter 4.

CHAPTER 4

1. An excellent introductory review of early dream theories

can be found in MacKenzie, *Dreams and Dreaming*, 1965. A more advanced review is that by de Becker, *The Understanding of Dreams,* 1968.

2. These dreams are prospective in the sense that they arise from the dreamer's past, and from an intellectual and physical capability to expand one's range of expression into new adult forms.

3. There is ample evidence that children's dreams alter from almost nonsymbolic expressions of feeling to indirect, symbolic withholdings of feelings as they get older. See Foulkes et al., 1969, and Van de Castle, 1970. There is also evidence that the way children talk about their feelings becomes more and more abstract and impersonal as they get older and learn the adult forms of nonexpression. See Lewis et al., 1971.

4. Consult A. H. Maslow, *Motivation and Personality,* New York: Harper & Row, 1954, for a discussion of his important paradigmatic experiments on peak experiences.

5. In psychotherapy research, many researchers have tried to bring out the difference between content assessments and process assessments. But this potentially valuable distinction has usually been misapplied because the researchers do not clearly identify the essential process variable in psychotherapy. An important simplification results once it is recognized that all process movement is essentially movement from defensiveness to expressiveness, from affect withholding to affect completion.

6. Both Reich, 1949, and Ferenczi, 1969, made major advances in psychoanalytic technique by stressing that character traits are as much a part of analytic scrutiny as the content of dreams, slips, memories and free associations. Unfortunately their advances were never generally accepted nor were they extended to apply to the dreamer's emotional traits. If Reich and Ferenczi had made this extension, they would have shifted psychoanalysis from the interpretive to the functional orientation to dreams.

CHAPTER 5

1. The result was eventually more symbolism, not less. But if

we closely examine the *process* of Jung, we can see him searching in the past for the community he needed in the present. He found the missing requirement — the collective — the sharing, but he didn't find it where he could live it — in his or his patients' present life. For two very good modern biographical accounts of Jung's life consult Hannah, 1976 and van der Post, 1975.

2. Perls also owes much, in his methods of therapy, to psychodrama (consult Greenberg, 1974), and in his theory, to Reich's formulations of character analysis (see Reich, 1949). However, Perls was a creative borrower who combined these influences in a unique way.

3. The same critique can be made of psychodrama as a method — too much emphasis is placed on the content and staging of the psychodrama.

4. As an aside it is interesting to comment here on the connections between the gestalt school of psychology and the Gestalt Therapy of Perls, and on the functional school of psychology and our Functional Therapy. In both, there is an emphasis that is carried over from the general school to the therapeutic application of the school. Perls applied the ideas of perceptual wholeness and foreground/background to the emotions and to dreams. In functional psychology (as seen in the work of Darwin and Dewey), there is an emphasis on the pragmatic, on what works, and there is an equal emphasis on subjective mediators of behavior (stream of consciousness). Applying these two emphases of functional psychology to therapy and to dreams results in a kind of pragmatic subjectivity. In the functional approach to dreams we want to stress, first, "How does the dreamer feel?" and second, "How does the dreamer function to influence his or own feelings?" It would take us too far afield to explore these connections among functional psychology, Functional Therapy, and functional dream analysis here. We intend to develop these ideas further in future books.

5. We refer interested readers to Caligor and May, *Dreams and Symbols*, 1968, and Rossi, *Dreams and the Growth of Personality*, 1972.

CHAPTER 6

1. Of course, this attitude is exactly the attitude of psychotherapy, but it has not been extended in modern day practice to therapeutic communities.

2. For a sampling of writings about other groups, see Lincoln, 1935; Middleton, 1967; Underhill, 1968; Densmore, 1941; Devereux, 1969; Driver, 1969; Roheim, 1945, 1950; Willoya and Brown, 1962; Kroeber and Heizer, 1967; and Egan, 1955. The only active present-day American Indian dream group that we know about is that of the Pomo Indians of Northern California. For information about them, see Brown and Andrews, 1969; Forbes, 1969; and Oswalt, 1964.

3. "Semai (Central Sakai) in northwestern Pahang and southern Perak; the Temiar (Temer, Northern Sakai, Seroq, Ple) in northern Perak and southern Kelantan; and the Jah Hut and Che Wong (Siwang, Beri Chuba), both just south of the main body of the Semai." From Lebar, Mickey, and Musgrave, *Ethnic Groups of Mainland Southeast Asia,* MRAF, 1964, p. 176.

4. Some recent popular books: Faraday, *Dream Power,* 1972; *The Dream Game,* 1974; and Garfield, *Creative Dreaming,* 1974 have failed to understand this point. Without this perspective on what is most basic, it is easy to be misled into a search for power dreams or lucid dreams and to focus on dream manipulation. Be clear that the functional approach to dreams does *not* encourage the conscious control of dreams through pre-sleep suggestions. Recent research has demonstrated that such methods of dream control do not work. See Foulkes and Griffin, 1976.

CHAPTER 7

1. Dr. Milton Kramer, Director of Research at the V.A. Hospital in Cincinnati, reported at a 1977 conference on sleep, that the most significant factor affecting overnight mood changes is the number of people present in the dreamer's dreams. The more people in a dream, the more up or happy the dreamer is likely to feel in the morning. "Being alone, even in your dreams, is not much fun,"

said Dr. Kramer. From the functional perspective this finding makes good sense since the dreamer cannot function with much emotional effectiveness if there is no one in his or her dreams to whom he or she can express feelings.

We have found in our own research (as discussed in the *Appendix*) that as the dreamer's functional dynamics increase so too does the realism and contact in his or her dreams. Dreaming, like living, becomes full of real contacts with real people in real ways.

2. Refer to Chapter 6 on the democratization of myth making.

CHAPTER 8

1. See *Appendix* for further clarification of these processes and the scales used to rate them.

2. The transcript is edited from a two-hour psychotherapy session in order to focus on the process described. See Hart, Corriere, and Binder, *Going Sane: An Introduction to Feeling Therapy,* New York: Dell Publishing Co., 1976, for more detailed analyses of the therapy process.

3. The therapist is neither directive nor nondirective; he is *responsive,* and that can involve extremes of both direction and nondirection. The concern with directiveness or nondirectiveness is a false issue that comes from a failure to discriminate between self-reports and self-expression. The therapist who is responsive must do everything he can to move a person from reporting to expressing— this can include extremes of directiveness. But when a patient is expressing his feelings, the therapist need only be present to help him stay with the feeling. He sustains but does not direct the feeling expression.

CHAPTER 9

1. We thank Konni Corriere (the therapist in this session) for providing this transcript and comments which were edited for reproduction in this chapter.

2. The transformative dream could be described as a psychologically more fit dream while the typical symbolic dream is a psycho-

logically less fit dream. See Binder et al., 1979; Corriere and Hart, 1979, and Karle et al., 1978 for discussions of the general psychological fitness model as a new approach to defining psychological health.

CHAPTER 10

1. Consult Carl Sagan, *The Dragons of Eden,* for an interesting general discussion of the place of affect in the evolution of human intelligence. For a more technical discussion read MacClean, *The Triune Concept of Brain and Behaviour,* 1973.

2. Of course, it would be very desirable to use the mass media to teach new cultural norms of feeling and expression. Even though these norms would be taught at the level of images, they would help prepare the viewer for contact teaching.

3. We are not alone in looking back to Darwin to find the roots of the functional approach. He is considered an early functionalist or "antecedent influence" by Schulz. See Schulz, *A History of Modern Psychology,* New York: Academic Press, 1960. See also John Dewey.

4. Two contemporary psychologists who have followed Darwin's conceptualizations are Tompkins, 1962, 1963, and Ekman, 1973. Of these two investigators, Tompkin's work is more closely related to our own. Ekman has conducted a long series of very careful experiments on emotion and the face but, in our view, his work is hampered by self-imposed restrictions within the behavioristic paradigm, e.g., "We have avoided the phrase 'facial expressions of emotion,' since it implies that some inner state is being manifest or shown externally, or that the behavior is intended to transmit information. Instead we have used the more awkward phrase, 'face and emotion' or 'facial behavior.'" From Ekman, 1973, p. 3. The implications that Ekman avoids are exactly the ones that we believe must be made.

5. For more information about the functional analysis of dreams see the *Appendix.* For more information about the general concept and methods of psychological fitness see Corriere and Hart, *Psychological Fitness,* 1979.

ADDITIONAL READINGS ON THE FUNCTIONAL APPROACH TO DREAMS

In this book we stress theories, clinical observations and clinical applications. However, the functional approach to dreams does have important research applications.

We have applied the functional approach to general psychological studies of dreams as well as to investigations of psychophysiological processes. A partial listing of articles and papers which report on our dream and sleep research is listed below:

PUBLISHED DREAM ARTICLES

1. Corriere, R., Hart J., Karle, W., Binder, J., Gold, S., & Woldenberg, L. Toward a new theory of dreaming, *Journal of Clinical Psychology*, 1977, 33(3), 807-19.

2. Hartshorn, K., Corriere, R., Karle, W., Switzer, A., Hart, J., Gold, S., & Binder, J. A re-application of the process scoring system for dreams. *Journal of Clinical Psychology*, 1977, 33(3), 844-48.

3. Corriere, R., Hart, J., Karle, W., Switzer, A., & Woldenberg, L. Application of the process scoring system to waking, dream and therapy reports. *Journal of Clinical Psychology*, 1978, 34(3), 700-706.

4. Karle, W., Hart, J., Corriere, R., & Woldenberg, L. *The Functional Analysis of Dreams: A New Theory of Dreaming.* Journal of Clinical Psychology Monograph Publications, 1979.

5. Karle, W., Corriere, R., & Hart, J. (Eds.) *Dream Research Newsletter,* 1978, 1(1-3). Published by The Center Foundation.

PUBLISHED DREAM PRESENTATIONS

1. Woldenberg, L. The Functional Theory of Dreaming. In J. Hart (Chair.), *The Functional Approach to Dreams.* Symposium presented at the meeting of the California State Psychological Association, Los Angeles, 1977.

2. Corriere, R. The Functional Approach to Dreams in Psychotherapy. In J. Hart (Chair.), *The Functional Approach to Dreams.* Symposium presented at the meeting of the California State Psychological Association, Los Angeles, 1977.

3. Karle, W. A Comparison of the Dreams of Patients and Non-Patients—Evidence for the Functional Approach. In J. Hart (Chair.), *The Functional Approach to Dreams.* Symposium presented at the meeting of the California State Psychological Association, Los Angeles, 1977.

4. Corriere, R. The Transformation of Dreams in Feeling Therapy. In J. Hart (Chair.), *Psychological and Psychophysiological Studies of Feeling Therapy.* Symposium presented at the meeting of the Western Psychological Association, Los Angeles, 1976.

5. Cirincione, D., Karle, W., & Woldenberg, L. Dreams in the Functional Approach to Psychotherapy. Paper presented at the American Association for Social Psychiatry, Santa Barbara, 1977.

6. Karle, W., Switzer, A., & Cirincione, D. A Modern Dreamer Community. Paper presented at the meeting of the Association for Humanistic Psychology, Toronto, 1978.

7. Karle, W., Corriere, R., Hart, J., & Switzer, A. Process Scoring of Waking, Dream and Therapy Reports. Paper discussed at the meeting of the Society for Psychotherapy Research, Toronto, 1978.

8. Gold, S. & Karle, W. A Modern Dreamer Community. Paper presented at the meeting of the California State Psychological Association, San Francisco, 1978.

9. Corriere, R., Karle, W., & Hart, J. Applications of the Process Scoring System to Waking, Dream and Therapy Reports. Poster presentation at the meeting of the Association for the Psychophysiological Study of Sleep, Palo Alto, 1978.

10. Hartshorn, K., Corriere, R., Karle, W., & Hart, J. Re-Application of the Process Scoring System for Dreams. Poster presentation at the meeting of the Association for the Psychophysiological Study of Sleep, Palo Alto, 1978.

PUBLISHED SLEEP ARTICLES

1. Karle, W., Hopper, M., Corriere, R., Hart, J., & Switzer, A. Two preliminary studies on sleep and psychotherapy. *Physiology and Behavior,* 1977, 19(3), 419-23.

2. Scott, R., Karle, W., Switzer, A., Hart, J., Corriere, R., & Woldenberg, L. Psychophysiological correlates of the spontaneous K-complex. *Perceptual and Motor Skills,* 1978, 46, 271-87.

PUBLISHED SLEEP ABSTRACTS

1. Corriere, R., Hart, J., Karle, W., & Woldenberg, L. Toward a new theory of dreaming. In Chase, M. H., Mitler, M. M. & Walter, P. L. (Eds.) *Sleep Research,* Vol. 6 BIS/BRI, UCLA, Los Angeles, 1977, 121.

2. Karle, W. & Hopper, M. Longitudinal changes in sleep patterns of patients. In Chase, M. H., Mitler, M. M., & Walter, P. L. (Eds.) *Sleep Research,* Vol. 6. BIS/BRI, UCLA, Los Angeles, 1977, 149.

3. Karle, W. & Scott, R. K—Complex changes in the sleep records of patients. In Chase, M. H., Mitler, M. M. & Walter, P. L. (Eds.) *Sleep Research,* Vol. 6, BIS/BRI, UCLA, Los Angeles, 1977, 151.

4. Karle, W., Hopper, M., Corriere, R., & Hart, J. The alteration of sleep patterns in psychotherapy. In Chase, M. H., Mitler, M. M. & Walter, P. L. (Eds.) *Sleep Research,* Vol. 6, BIS/BRI, UCLA, Los Angeles, 1977, 150.

5. Karle, W. & Hopper, M. Two preliminary studies on sleep and psychotherapy. *Psychophysiology,* 15 (3), 1978, 273.

6. Scott, R., Hopper, M., & Karle, W. Psychophysiological correlates of the spontaneous K-complex. *Psychophysiology,* 15 (3), 1978, 273.

PUBLISHED SLEEP PRESENTATIONS

1. Karle, W. & Hopper, M. Longitudinal Changes in Sleep Patterns of Patients. Paper presented at the meeting of the Association for the Psychophysiological Study of Sleep, Houston, April, 1977.

2. Karle, W. & Hopper, M. The Alteration of Sleep Patterns in Psychotherapy. Paper at the meeting of the Association for the Psychophysiological Study of Sleep, Houston, April, 1977.

3. Karle, W. & Scott, R. K-Complex Changes in the Sleep Records of Patients. Paper presented at the meeting of the Association for the Psychophysiological Study of Sleep, Houston, April, 1977.

4. Hopper, M. The Effects of Psychotherapy on EEG Sleep Patterns. In W. Karle (Chair.), *Psychophysiological Changes Associated with Different Periods of Experience in Psychotherapy.* Symposium presented at the meeting of the California State Psychological Association, Los Angeles, 1977.

5. Scott, R. Psychophysiological Correlates of the Spontaneous K-Complex. In W. Karle (Chair.), *Psychophysiological Changes Associated wtih Different Periods of Experience in Psychotherapy.* Symposium presented at the meeting of the California State Psychological Association, Los Angeles, 1977.

6. Karle, W. Psychotherapy and Sleep: A Case Study. In J. Hart (Chair.), *Psychological and Psychophysiological Studies of Feeling Therapy.* Symposium presented at the meeting of the Western Psychological Association, Los Angeles, 1976.

7. Karle, W. & Hopper, M. Two Preliminary Studies on Sleep and Psychotherapy. Display and discussion presentation at the meeting of the Society for Psychophysiological Research, Philadelphia, 1977.

8. Scott, R., Hopper, M., & Karle, W. Psychophysiological Correlates of the Spontaneous K-Complex. Display and discussion presentation at the meeting of the Society for Psychophysiological Research, Philadelphia, 1977.

9. Karle, W., Corriere, R., Hart, J., & Hopper, M. Effects of Psychotherapy on REM Time and REM Latency. Display and discussion presentation at the meeting of the Society for Psychophysiological Research, Madison, 1978.

10. Karle, W., Corriere, R., & Hart, J. Do Relaxed Psychotherapy Patients Really Fall Asleep More Easily? A report on subjective sleep latency. Poster presentation at the meeting of the Association for the Psychophysiological Study of Sleep, Palo Alto, 1978.

DOCTORAL DISSERTATIONS AND MASTERS THESES

1. Cammer, S. Applying the Functional Approach to Dreams: A Clinical and Personal Study. Masters Thesis, Fielding Institute, Santa Barbara, 1978.

2. Corriere, R. The Transformation of Dreams, Ph.D. Thesis, University of California, Irvine, 1975.

3. Gold, N. A Study of Dreams and How They Change. Masters Thesis, California State University, Northridge, 1976.

4. Karle, W. A New Orientation for Sleep Research: Sleep and Psychotherapy. Ph. D. Thesis, University of California, Irvine, 1975.

5. McEuen, D. A New Approach to Dreams and Waking Experience. Masters Thesis, California State University, Northridge, 1976.

6. Hartshorn, K. A New Dimension in Dreaming. Master's Thesis, California State University, Northridge, 1976.

7. Hopper, M. When Dreams Change: Sleep in Psychotherapy. Ph.D. Thesis, University of California, Irvine, 1976.

8. Scott, R. Sleep and the K-Complex. Ph.D. Thesis, University of California, Irvine, 1976.

For a full listing of current research related to the functional approach to counseling and psychotherapy write to:

Research Coordinator
The Center Foundation
7165 Sunset Boulevard
Los Angeles, California 90046

For a listing of professional training programs on the functional approach to dreams, counseling and psychotherapy, and psychological fitness write to:

Program Coordinator
The Center for Functional Psychotherapy
7165 Sunset Boulevard
Los Angeles, California 90046

BIBLIOGRAPHY

Abbott, E.A. *Flatland.* 7th Edition. New York: Dover Publications, Inc., 1952.

Binder, J., Karle, W., Corriere, R., Hart, J. & Richard, A. "A New Model for Professionals: Psychological Fitness Training," *Canadian Journal of Mental Hygiene,* 1979.

Boss, M. *The Analysis of Dreams.* London: Rider, 1958.

Boss, M. *Psychoanalysis and Daseinalysis.* New York: Basic Books, 1963.

Boss, M. *"I Dreamt Last Night . . ."* New York: Gardner Press, 1977.

Brown, V. & Andrews, D. *The Pomo Indians of California and Their Neighbors.* Healdsburg, California: Naturegraph Company, 1969.

Caligor, L. & May, R. *Dreams and Symbols: Man's Unconscious Language.* New York: Basic Books, 1968.

Campbell, J. *The Masks of God: Primitive Mythology.* New York: Viking Press, 1959.

Campbell, J. *The Masks of God: Creative Mythology.* New York: Viking Press, 1968.

Clynes, M. *Sentics: The Touch of Emotions.* New York: Doubleday, 1977.

Corriere, R. & Hart, J. *The Dream Makers.* New York: Funk and Wagnalls, 1977.

Corriere, R. & Hart, J. *Psychological Fitness.* New York: Harcourt Brace Jovanovich, 1979.

Corriere, R., Hart, J., Karle, W., Binder, J., Gold, S., & Woldenberg, L. "Toward a New Theory of Dreaming," *Journal of Clinical Psychology*, 1977, 33 (3), 807-19.

Curtis, N. *The Indian's Book*. New York: Dover Publications, 1950.

Darwin, C. *The Expression of the Emotions in Man and Animals*. Chicago and London: The University of Chicago Press, 1965.

de Becker, R. *The Understanding of Dreams*. New York: Hawthorn Books, 1968.

Densmore, F. *The Study of Indian Music*. 3rd Edition. Smithsonian Report, 1941.

Dentan, R.K. *The Semai, a Nonviolent People of Malaysia*. New York: Holt, Rinehart and Winston, 1968.

Devereux, G. *Reality and Dream: Psychotherapy of a Plains Indian*. Garden City, New York: Doubleday and Co., (Anchor Books), 1969.

Driver, H.E. *Indians of North America*. 2nd Edition, revised. Chicago: University of Chicago Press, 1969.

Egan. D. "The Personal Use of Myth in Dreams." *Journal of American Folklore*, 1955, 68, 445-53.

Ekman, P. (Ed.) *Darwin and Facial Expression*. New York: Academic Press, 1973.

Faraday, A. *Dream Power*. New York: Berkeley Medallion, 1972.

Faraday, A. *The Dream Game*. New York: Harper and Row, 1974.

Ferenczi, S. *Further Contributions to the Theory and Technique of Psychoanalysis*. London: Hogarth Press, 1969.

Forbes, J. *Native Americans of California and Nevada*. Healdsburg, California: Naturegraph Publishers, 1969.

Foulkes, D. *The Psychology of Sleep*. New York: Charles Scribner's Sons, 1966.

Foulkes, D., Larson, J.D., Swanson, E.M., & Rardin, M. "Two Studies of Childhood Dreaming." *American Journal of Orthopsychiatry*, 1969, 39, 627-43.

Foulkes, D. *What Do We Know About Dreams and How Did We Learn It?* Paper presented at the meeting of the Association for the Psychophysiological Study of Sleep, San Diego, 1973.

Foulkes, D. & Griffin, M.L. "An Experimental Study of Creative Dreaming," *Sleep Research, BIS/BRI,* 1976, 5, 129.

Freud, S. *A General Introduction to Psychoanalysis.* New York: Permabook, 1953.

Freud, S. *The Interpretation of Dreams.* New York: Basic Books, 1960.

Freud, S. *New Introductory Lectures.* J. Strachey (Trans.), New York: W.W. Norton, 1965.

Gardiner, M. (Ed.) *The Wolf Man.* New York: Basic Books, Inc., 1971.

Garfield, P. *Creative Dreaming.* New York: Simon and Schuster, 1974.

Gendlin, E.T. *Experiencing and the Creation of Meaning.* Glencoe, Illinois: Free Press, 1962.

Greenberg, I.A. (Ed.) *Psychodrama: Theory and Therapy.* New York: Behavioral Publications, 1974.

Hall, C. "What People Dream About," *Scientific American,* 1951, 184, 60-63.

Hall, C. & Nordby, V. *The Individual and His Dreams.* New York: Signet Books, 1972.

Hall, C. & Van de Castle, R. *The Content Analysis of Dreams.* New York: Appleton-Century-Crofts, 1966.

Hannah, B. *Jung: His Life and Work.* New York: G.P. Putnam's Sons, 1976.

Harlow, H. "Manipulation Drive," *Journal of Experimental Psychology,* 1950, 40, 228-34.

Harlow, H. *Learning to Love.* New York: Ballantine Books, 1971.

Hart, J. "Dreams in the Classroom," *Experiment and Innovation,* 1971, IV (1), 51-66.

Hart, J. "Questions and Answers about Feeling Therapy and the Functional School of Psychotherapy," *Center Newsletter,* 1977, 1(6), 5.

Hart, J., Corriere, R., & Binder, J. *Going Sane.* New York: Aronson, 1975; Delta Paperback (Dell), 1976.

Hartshorn, K., Corriere, R., Karle, W., Switzer, A., Hart, J., Gold, S., & Binder, J. "A Reapplication of the Process Scoring System for Dreams," *Journal of Clinical Psychology,* 1977, 33 (3), 844-48.

Hunter, W. S. "Conditioning and Extinction in the Rat," *British Journal of Psychology,* 1935, 26, 135-45.

Idris, J.B. *A Brief Note on the Orang Asli of West Malaysia and Their Administration.* Department of Orang Asli Affairs, Ministry of National and Rural Development, Malaysia, 1972, p. 4.

Jung, C. *The Archetypes of the Collective Unconscious.* Bollingen Series XX. Princeton: Princeton University Press, 1968.

Jung, C. *Memories, Dreams, Reflections.* New York: Vintage, 1961.

Jung, C. *Dreams.* Bollingen Series. Princeton: Princeton University Press, 1974.

Kardiner, A. *My Analysis with Freud.* New York: Norton, 1977.

Karle, W., Corriere, R., Hart, J., Gold, S., Maple, C., & Hopper, M. "Maintenance of Psychophysiological Changes in Feeling Therapy." *Psychological Reports,* 1976, 39, 1143-47.

Karle, W., Hopper, M., Corriere, R., Hart, J., & Switzer, A. "Two Preliminary Studies on Sleep and Psychotherapy." *Physiology and Behavior,* 1977, 19 (3), 419-23.

Karle, W., Globus, G., Phoebus, E., Hart, J., & Corriere, R. "The Occurrence of Dreams and Its Relation to REM Periods." In M. Chase, W. Stern & P. Walter (Eds.), *Sleep Research,* Vol. 1. Los Angeles: Brain Information Service, 1972, 106.

Karle, W., Switzer, A., Gold, S., & Binder, J. "A New Model for

Continuing Affective Education," *Canadian Journal of University Continuing Education,* 1978, Vol. V, 35-39.

Karle, W., Woldenberg, L., & Hart, J. Feeling Therapy: Transformation in Psychotherapy. In V. Binder, A. Binder, & B. Rimland (Eds.), *Modern Therapies.* New York: Prentice-Hall, 1976.

Kroeber, T. & Heizer, R.F. *Almost Ancestors: The First Californians.* New York: Sierra Club — Ballantine Books, 1967.

Lebar, L., Mickey, M., & Musgrave, R. *Ethnic Groups of Mainland Southeast Asia.* M.R.A.F., 1964.

Lewis, W.C., Wolman, R.N., & King, M. "The Development of the Language of Emotions." *American Journal of Psychiatry,* 1971, 127, 1491-97.

Liddick, B. "Going Sane Around the Clock." Los Angeles: *Los Angeles Times,* June 13, 1976.

Lincoln, J.S. *The Dream in Primitive Cultures.* London: Cresset Press, 1935.

London, P. *Modes and Morals of Psychotherapy.* New York: Holt, Rinehart and Winston, 1964.

MacKenzie, N. *Dreams and Dreaming.* New York: Vanguard Press, 1965.

MacLean, P.D. *The Triune Concept of the Brain and Behavior.* Toronto: University of Toronto Press, 1973.

Maslow, A.H. *Motivation and Personality.* New York: Harper and Row, 1954.

Meier, C.A. *Ancient Incubation and Modern Psychotherapy.* Evanston, Illinois: Northwestern University Press, 1967.

Middleton, J. (Ed.) *Magic, Witchcraft, and Curing.* Garden City, New York: Natural History Press, 1967.

Miller, G.A., Galanter, E., & Pribram, K.H. *Plans and the Structure of Behavior.* New York: Holt, Rinehart and Winston, 1960.

Noone, H.D. *Temiar Dream Songs from Malaya.* New York: Ethnic Folkways Library, 1955. Album and Album Notes No. P460, p. 3.

Noone, R. & Holman, D. *In Search of the Dream People.* New York: William Morrow, 1972.

Oswalt, R. *Kashaya Texts.* Berkeley: University of California Publications in Linguistics, Vol. 36. University of California Press, 1964.

Perls, F. *In and Out the Garbage Pail.* Lafayette, California: Real People Press, 1969.

Perls, F. *Gestalt Therapy Verbatim.* Lafayette, California: Real People Press, 1969.

Pribram, K.H. *Languages of the Brain.* Englewood Cliffs, New Jersey: Prentice Hall, 1971.

Reich, W. *Character Analysis.* 3rd Edition. New York: Farrar, Straus, and Giroux, 1949.

Relander, C. *Drummers and Dreamers.* Caldwell, Idaho: The Caxton Printers, Ltd., 1957.

Roheim, G. *The Eternal Ones of the Dream.* New York: International Universities Press, 1945.

Roheim, G. *Psychoanalysis and Anthropology: Culture, Personality and the Unconscious.* New York: International Universities Press, 1950.

Rossi, E.H. *Dreams and the Growth of Personality.* New York: Pergamon Press, 1972.

Sagan, C. *The Dragons of Eden.* New York: Random House, 1977.

Schultz, D.P. *A History of Modern Psychology.* New York: Academic Press, 1960.

Shontz, F.C. *Research Methods in Personality.* New York: Meredith Publishing Corp., 1965.

Stewart, K. "The Dream Comes of Age," *Mental Hygiene,* 1962, 46, 230–36.

Stewart, K. *Magico-religious beliefs and practices in primitive society —a sociological interpretation of their therapeutic aspects.* Unpublished doctoral dissertation, London School of Economics, 1947.

Stewart, K. "Mental Hygiene and World Peace." *Mental Hygiene,* July, 1954, XXXVIII (3), 401.

Stewart, K. "Dream Theory in Malaya." In C. Tart (Ed.), *Altered States of Consciousness.* New York: John Wiley & Sons, 1969, 159-67.

Tart, C. *Altered States of Consciousness.* New York: John Wiley and Sons, 1969.

Tompkins, S. *Affect, Imagery, Consciousness.* Vols. I & II. New York: Springer, 1962-1963.

Trossman, H., Rechtschaffen, A., Offenkrantz, W., & Wolpert, E. "Studies in Psychophysiology of Dreams." *Archives of General Psychiatry,* 1960, 3, 51.

Underhill, R.M. *Singing for Power.* Berkeley: University of California Press, 1968.

Van de Castle, R. L. "His, Hers and the Children's Dreams." *Psychology Today,* 1970, 4 (1), 37-39.

van der Post, L. *Jung and the Story of Our Time.* New York: Pantheon Books, 1975.

Wallace, A. "Dreams and Wishes of the Soul: A Type of Psychoanalytic Theory among Seventeenth Century Iroquois." In J. Middleton (Ed.) *Magic, Witchcraft and Curing.* Garden City, New York: National History Press, 1967.

Webster's New World Dictionary of the American Language. Cleveland and New York: The College World Publishing Company, 1957.

Weisz, R. & Foulkes, D. "Home and Laboratory Dreams Collected under Uniform Sampling Conditions." *Psychophysiology,* 1970, 6, 588-96.

White, T. "Motivation Reconsidered," *Psychological Review,* 1959, 66, 297-333.

Willoya, W. & Brown, V. *Warriors of the Rainbow.* Healdsburg, California: Naturegraph Company, 1962.

Woldenberg, L., Karle, W., Gold, S., Corriere, R., Hart, J., &

Hopper, M. "Psychophysiological Changes in Feeling Therapy." *Psychological Reports*, 1976, 39, 1059-62.

Wyss, D. *Depth Psychology: A Critical History.* New York: W.W. Norton and Company, Inc., 1966.

INDEX